Northern Roots

Rod Broome

ISIS
LARGE PRINT
Oxford

First published in Great Britain 2007
by
Isis Publishing Ltd.

Published in Large Print 2007 by ISIS Publishing Ltd.,
7 Centremead, Osney Mead, Oxford OX2 0ES
by arrangement with
the Author

British Library Cataloguing in Publication Data
Broome, Rod, 1937–
   Northern roots. – Large print ed.
   (Isis reminiscence series)
   1. Broome, Rod, 1937– – Childhood and youth
   2. Large type books
   3. Lancashire (England) – Biography
   I. Title
   942.7'6084'092

ISBN 978–0–7531–9398–3 (hb)
ISBN 978–0–7531–9399–0 (pb)

Printed and bound in Great Britain by
T. J. International Ltd., Padstow, Cornwall

B=BRO

Northern Roots

Acknowledgements

My grateful thanks to my wife Anita, for her encouragement and patience in reading and re-reading my manuscript, making helpful suggestions and correcting errors, and the staff at Isis for leading me gently and efficiently through all the processes involved in the publication of this book.

Introduction

Many of us have seen television documentaries in which, as a sequence of events is shown, the caption "RECONSTRUCTION" appears at the foot of the screen. When this happens, we know that what we are watching is not a film of an original happening. Someone has collected as much information as possible about a particular event and portrayed to the best of their ability what they believe took place. We, as viewers, cannot be certain of the accuracy of what we see, but we know that if the film-maker has integrity, the reconstruction will not be too far from the truth.

When it comes to remembering episodes from our own life, however, we feel certain we are watching an "original film". We see past occurrences replayed in our mind's eye — and convince ourselves that they represent a totality of truth. Not so. What we are watching is a reconstruction. Information has been stored in our memory and put together to form a story — but it is full of flaws and inconsistencies. One only has to hear a description of a football match from the supporters of opposing teams to know the truth of this.

In the account that follows I have done my best to portray things as they really were, but one has to remember that I saw most of the events and situations I describe through the eyes of a child. Also, it has to be remembered that every viewpoint is a view from a point, and I cannot be certain that some episodes are not viewed through rose-tinted spectacles and others with a jaundiced eye.

The names of the places, family members and other adults in my account have been recorded accurately (as far as I know), but one or two of the children's names have been changed to protect the innocent!

CHAPTER
ONE

The One and Only

Children were a rarity in my family. When James Arnold Broome, cobbler of this parish, married Hilda Ackroyd, employee of Beswick's Pickle Factory, at Greenhill Primitive Methodist Chapel on 2nd October 1935, there were none present at the wedding. The celebratory photograph reveals a row of seven smiling adults in formal pose, gazing into the camera lens.

Let me introduce them to you.

In the centre of the picture stands the happy couple: Dad, tall and handsome, wearing circular spectacles and white kid gloves, defying anyone to guess that he's a humble cobbler, and Mum, slim and elegant, looking more like a debutante than a pickle packer.

On the left of the photograph, demure and pretty in her bridesmaid's dress is Nellie, Dad's youngest sister, and on the right in a matching gown, Olive, Mum's only sister.

Escorting these two beauties are Tom, Olive's "intended", and Charlie, best man and Dad's elder brother.

The older man at Mum's side is her father, whom she referred to as her "Dada" until the day that she died.

1

Of course, several guests attended the ceremony who do not appear on the photograph. There was Mum's mother, the fourth and final member of the Ackroyd family, and Dad's parents and his remaining sisters, Annie and Florence.

There may well have been others but if there were, they were all adults. There were no children. And strange as it may seem, there were to be no children, for amongst all their siblings, Mum and Dad were the only family members to become parents. Olive and Tom eventually married but remained childless, as did Charlie and his wife, Ethel. Nellie and Florence never married, and Annie was beyond childbearing years by the time she found a partner.

So when I arrived on the scene on 6th August 1937, the first-born son of Hilda and Arnold (Dad was never known as James), there is little doubt that I would have been the focus of all attention.

Looking back, I have a mental picture of the family network at the time resembling a spider's web with myself at the centre. It seemed natural to be surrounded by a host of attentive adults who talked to me, played with me and bought me presents. Although I was born two years before the outbreak of the Second World War, I didn't suffer the childhood deprivation experienced by many of my contemporaries. I had all the food I needed and was given a lot of toys — bought mainly by relatives who were kind enough to spend their pocket money on me. I didn't think it unusual that I had no cousins or that there were no other children in the family. I just took it all in my stride.

★　★　★

I was born at number 33 Calderbrook Road, a rented, two-up-two-down stone cottage at the end of a row, about half a mile from the centre of Littleborough in Lancashire in a locality known as "Laneside". In front of the house was a small garden — and at the side of it a field which was often full of cows.

In spite of its very basic facilities, our house was superior to many others in the neighbourhood. To begin with, our front door did not open directly on to the pavement and we were doubly protected from the dust of the road by a vestibule in the corner of the front room. The kitchen was small, but had been updated a little with a porcelain sink — with cold tap — under the window, and we also had a large attic that could be reached by a proper staircase rather than through a trapdoor. From a corner of the kitchen a flight of stone steps led down into a coal cellar which, although dark and damp, was a useful place to store our tin bath, some boxes of Dad's tools, and baskets of Mum's vegetables. As well as coal, of course.

Our greatest benefit, however, but one which I did not fully appreciate at the time, was a flushing lavatory in a brick building only a few strides from our back door. Many other houses in the area had "tub-toilets", which gradually filled up as the days went by and were emptied weekly by a group of council workmen who trundled around the streets with a wagon. So we were very fortunate.

Mind you, the toilet block was not for our exclusive use. Our house was the end one in a row of five with a communal back yard, and the brick building containing three separate lavatories and an open-fronted alcove housing five dustbins was shared by all.

The arrangement was that the first toilet was used by ourselves from number 33 and number 29, the second toilet was used only by number 31, and the third by numbers 27 and 25. How such an arrangement came about I do not know, but it meant that quite often, whilst performing, one was interrupted by the next-door-but-one neighbours. As there was no lock on the door, one became adept at sitting with a leg sticking straight out in front to repel invaders, and a readiness to call "Hello!" as soon as footsteps were heard on the stone flags outside.

There were some disadvantages to a water closet, however. It took quite a bit of looking after. Once a year, our next-door-but-one neighbours and ourselves took it in turns to whitewash the inside of it, and every winter the strips of sacking lagging the pipe-work were checked or renewed. From October to March, a small paraffin "kelly" lamp was placed strategically under the water cistern to avoid a freeze-up, and of course there was the weekly job of threading squares of newspaper on to string and hanging them on a nail knocked into the mortar for the purpose.

However, harmony usually reigned between our neighbours and ourselves when it came to maintaining the toilet. They were, in fact, distantly related to us as the lady of the house was Mum's cousin and was actually referred to as "Cousin Marion" by us all throughout her life. So perhaps that's why there was such close co-operation.

Whilst on the subject of toilets, some local people were doubly disadvantaged, having both a tub toilet that was shared — and also having a long walk to get to it. Almost opposite to us on Laneside was a row containing about a dozen back-to-back houses. This meant they faced on to the road and had no back doors. They were matched by an identical set at the rear pointing in the opposite direction. The toilets for all these houses were in a block situated centrally round the back of the row. So when the neighbours opposite felt the call of nature they had to come out of their front (and only) doors, walk along the pavement to the end of the row, go round the back and then walk a similar distance to reach their destination. Imagine the frustration — and discomfort — if they arrived to find the lavatory already occupied! One neighbour in particular — a Mrs Oldroyd — caused my father considerable amusement by leaving her front door wearing slippers and making the journey round the block swinging a key attached to an empty cotton reel. He would look at me with a twinkle in his eye and ask, "Where do you think *she's* going?"

Given the inconvenience of such arrangements, it is hardly surprising that every household had a selection of chamber pots and buckets that could be used in inclement weather or at unsociable hours.

Some of my earliest memories centre on visiting "Grandma Broome's" house — a large terraced

5

property on Stubley Brow about a mile from my home. It seemed as though this place was a hive of activity — there was always something going on.

As well as Grandma and Grandad, my three maiden aunts lived there. The eldest was Annie, who was tall and slim like Grandma and had jet-black hair. She always seemed rather distant and aloof and played with me the least of the three. It came as an enormous shock when I discovered in my teens that her black hair was dyed, and had been for many a year, because it had turned prematurely white.

Then came Florence who was somewhat retarded and had a speech impediment. Although I was able to understand every word she said — as could all the family — many "outsiders" found her difficult to follow. For years, Florence bought me a weekly comic which I looked forward to eagerly every Friday night.

My parents used to relate an amusing story about Florence. As a cobbler, my father often held small nails (rivets) in his mouth, which he took out one by one and hammered into the sole of the shoe on his last. One day, Florence overheard him telling my mother that he thought he might have accidentally swallowed one, whereupon she returned to my grandparents' house and reported that "Arnold has swallowed a PRIVET!"

Lastly, there was Nellie, who was my favourite aunt. In contrast to the demure image on the wedding photograph, she was in fact loud and raucous, but as a child, I saw her as the centre of all fun. She would play games with me, take me out for walks and generally be as boisterous as a ten-year-old boy! I can still hear her laugh ringing out as she engaged in some infantile activity and I remember with affection the Christmas parties where she coerced the entire family of staid adults to participate in a series of games that were really only appropriate to children of five or six. The names of the games remain in my memory: "The Tingalary Man"; "Tippit"; "Lotto"; "Snap"; "Tell Me"; and many others. I am still not sure whether the first two in the list were universally known party games or whether they were unique to my family and Auntie Nellie.

One Easter during the War, when luxuries were scarce, Auntie Nellie took me aside.

"We're going to make some chocolate Easter eggs," she said. "I'll get everything ready, and you come and see me on Saturday afternoon."

I could hardly wait. I'd never seen an Easter egg.

When I arrived, there were several items spread over the scrubbed kitchen table. We tied on our aprons, washed our hands and got down to business. Putting a block of chocolate into a bowl and placing it over a pan of boiling water on the gas cooker, we waited for it to melt. After it had liquified, we poured it carefully into two well-greased eggcups. Then, when it had cooled, we removed it from the "moulds" and stuck the two halves together using more melted chocolate for the purpose.

I was the only child around to have an Easter egg that year, and I did not worry about the fact that it was solid, with a "waist" in the middle!

It was Auntie Nellie who composed the appalling little ditty that caused me so much embarrassment in my early years. Its inspiration was a photograph that had been taken of me when I was only a few weeks old. But this was no amateur snapshot; it was an "A. A. Budd" special. The local professional photographer had placed me, face down and naked, on a couch in his studio — and as I raised myself on my elbows and looked at him in surprise, he had pressed the button and created his masterpiece. All the relatives were given a copy and each was framed and placed in a position of honour.

When I was four or five, in case there was any doubt as to the identity of the naked baby who peered down from the top of bookcases and mantle-shelves wherever I went, Auntie Nellie provided an illuminating piece of doggerel:

"In Grandma's front room
There is a little boy
Who has no knick-knicks on.
And oh, his botty will be cold!"

This was followed by gales of kindly laughter and, after every scrap of amusement had been squeezed out of the episode, a repeat performance!

These then were the inhabitants of Grandma Broome's when I was a child. I did not find out until I was in my late teens that there had been another sister, Frances Emily, who was born between Annie and Florence, and who had come to an untimely end at the age of twenty-six. Although the story was never told in my company, over the years I gradually pieced together the main threads of it, and discovered what had happened to my missing aunt.

One evening, Frances had been to a Social at Stubley Methodist Chapel, which was just across the road from where she lived, but had not returned home afterwards. Searches had been instigated, and days later an S.O.S. message was broadcast on the radio, but despite all efforts she was not found. Although no-one could account for her sudden disappearance, several friends who had been with her during the evening said she had seemed very quiet and had complained of a headache.

Then, some three weeks later, a body was seen floating in the Rochdale Canal, close to a bridge, about a mile from the family home. My father had the unpleasant task of identifying the body of his sister Frances. She was fully clothed in the same garments in which she had attended the Social, and there were no signs of a struggle or an attack.

How she got there was never discovered. What actually happened we shall never know, but at the inquest held some time later, the coroner did not bring in a verdict of suicide, but recorded that she had been "found drowned".

Childless Charlie and Ethel, Dad's brother and sister-in-law, had set up home in a little redbrick terraced house in Whittle Street only a hundred yards from Grandma Broome's house, and it soon became clear to me that any visit to the latter must also include a visit to the former. If it were discovered that Mum or Dad — and later, myself — had been to one house without calling at the other, offence was immediately taken.

The house was in a row owned by Whittle's Bakery where both Ethel and Charlie worked, and it afforded much better accommodation than that enjoyed by many people of the time. To begin with, it had three rooms downstairs, a private yard and, luxury of luxuries, *a bathroom*.

My aunt and uncle's privileged existence provoked some jealousy amongst other members of the family who still had to put up with a tin bath in front of the fire — but to be fair, they made their modern facility available to all family members who wished to take advantage of it, provided they brought their own towel.

Looking back, there was always a slight antagonism between my parents (Mum in particular) and Ethel and Charlie, which I believe arose out of jealousy. Ethel and Charlie's house contained better quality furniture than other family members could afford and, as they both went out to work, their income was greater than that of my parents. As I grew older, I perceived dark hints that they had *chosen* not to have a family and had lived to regret it.

As an infant, I found my visits to Ethel and Charlie's house were never as entertaining as trips to Grandma Broome's. The good quality furniture meant I had to sit quietly whilst the adults talked, so I was usually bored within ten minutes of arriving. And yet, in many ways

Ethel was the most generous of all the relatives. She possessed a tin containing the most wonderful selection of biscuits — even chocolate-covered "Penguins" and "Blue Ribands" — and she always brought it out and let me take my pick when I called. And in spite of Mum's uncharitable suspicions, the house was often full of neighbours' children to whom she gave sweets and other treats. They may have flocked around her in response to bribes, but it was obvious that she wanted them to be there and enjoyed their company.

My memories of the Ackroyd household — my mother's parents — are not as clear as those of the Broomes, so I can only assume that either I did not go there as often or, more likely, the trips were not particularly memorable. Mum's parents did in fact live closer to us than the Broomes — indeed further along Calderbrook Road at number 123 — but I can recall few interesting episodes or encounters with them. Auntie Olive, Mum's younger sister, had married and been whisked away by Tom Doidge in 1936 before I was born, so whenever we visited the house, the older Ackroyds were the only occupants. This contrasted strongly with the Broome household, which usually contained three young women, one of whom was ready to embark upon any crazy escapade at the drop of a hat!

Nevertheless, it was to Grandad Ackroyd that I owed my early skill at the game of draughts. I remember, as a small boy, that he had a wooden draught-box which,

11

when opened, transformed itself into a chequered board.

"Now then," he would say when Mum and Grandma were chatting in the kitchen, "Let's see what we can do with this." And going to a cupboard in the sideboard he would take out the polished wooden box and walk over to the table with it. Having placed it between us on the heavy green cloth, he would set out his pieces and then wait for me to set out mine.

"Right," he would say, "it's black to start."

It was from Grandad Ackroyd that I learnt the opening moves of the game, the trick of never touching the back row of pieces until it was absolutely essential, the secret of avoiding defeat by using a "double corner", and the mysteries and powers of "crowners". He often let me win, but occasionally he would exercise his superiority by surrendering a single piece and then, as I watched in horror, leaping consecutively over four of my pieces.

I may not have been a match for Grandad Ackroyd, but throughout my childhood his teaching enabled me to make mincemeat of my contemporaries, and even today I still rate myself as a reasonably skilful player.

As I have said, I don't remember Auntie Olive ever living with my grandparents in Littleborough, but I do remember my first visit to see her as a small child. One Saturday morning, Mum and Dad told me we were going on a long journey.

"We're going on the Hebble bus," they said. "It's a single decker and it hardly ever stops. We're going to

Yorkshire!" So off we went to the centre of Littleborough where we waited at the special Hebble bus stop, near to the Parish Church. When the bus arrived we climbed aboard and our marathon began. Eventually, after a series of changes and several enquiries in various bus stations, we arrived at Bramley, near Leeds, less than forty miles away. And there, on a main road, we found what we were looking for — a sweets and tobacconist's shop which Olive and Tom had bought. It transpired that Olive had married into money, and that Tom's mother, who lived locally and actually owned a fur coat, had helped them with the purchase of the business.

It soon became apparent that Tom was his mother's son because following his demobilisation from the army where he served as a driver and an officer's batman, he became filled with a desire to make an even greater fortune. By the time I was eight, he had persuaded Olive that it would be very profitable to buy a hotel at a seaside resort and take in guests. So a year or two later they sold the sweet shop and bought the Kingsway Private Hotel on Valley Road in Scarborough.

Unfortunately it didn't quite work out as planned. Although Tom went to classes and eventually gained a City and Guilds certificate in catering, neither he nor Olive seemed to have the right attributes to make a success of the business. Tom's over-riding aim seemed to be to make money, and almost every conversation with him ended in a discussion about financial gain. This annoyed my father very much because when we went to stay with them Dad ended up paying for everyone if we went to the theatre, had ice creams, or travelled on a bus. Tom never seemed to have the right change in his pocket, or was slow at finding his money, or only happened to have a large value note.

Olive, on the other hand, began to have delusions of grandeur and modelled herself on Princess Margaret, whom she greatly admired. She wore fashionable clothes and flashy jewellery, and put on airs and graces which she believed gave the impression that she was one of the "upper class". Gradually, she developed a "posh" accent which she could not sustain, and continually revealed her working class roots by greeting her guests with:

"Ho, 'ello, 'ow are you? 'Ave you 'ad a henjoyable journey?"

Unfortunately, the impression she intended to convey was also somewhat marred by providing visitors with cheap sherry, or having polite (but heated) discussions with Tom about whose turn it was to hand around the cigarettes.

I seem to have few detailed memories of my early life at home with Mum and Dad. Certain isolated events rise like mountain peaks out of the mist but I cannot recall much of the daily routine in Calderbrook Road, or the pattern of interaction I had with my parents. I know that Mum cared for me at home, and I did not attend a nursery class or playgroup of any kind. I also have a clear memory of my favourite toy — "Cowboy" — an appropriately dressed doll who accompanied me to bed every night.

However, as I have grown older, two things in particular about my parents' relationship have become apparent to me. The first is the way in which they addressed each other. I can never, at any time, remember any words of love passing between them, any terms of endearment or pet names that showed affection. Not once did I overhear the word "darling" or "dearest" — or even the Lancashire "love". They were always "Hilda" and "Arnold" to each other, even when alone and embarrassment was not an issue.

The second thing that strikes me is the lack of physicality in their relationship. I cannot recall their ever putting their arms around each other or enjoying a cuddle. Even on the rare occasions when they met after being apart for some time, they did not greet each other with a kiss except, perhaps, for a peck on the cheek.

This is not to say they did not love each other. It has to be remembered that in the 1930s, 1940s and 1950s, extravagant expressions of affection were not as common as nowadays, particularly amongst the working classes. But it does strike me as odd that not once in twenty years did I witness a full-blown kiss or passionate embrace between them.

One consequence of their behaviour was that I, too, grew up unused to physical contact. I was very well cared-for and well-fed, but I didn't experience many hugs and kisses as a child. There were no spontaneous touchings or strokings; no running up to Mum or Dad and flinging one's arms round their necks or sitting on their knee; no cuddling up next to them and having a story read or told.

In retrospect, Mum does not seem to have been a naturally "warm" person, although I'm sure she thought she was. When I was much older, she would say, "Come and give your mother a kiss," and point to her cheek. She would seem genuinely hurt if I failed to comply with her request, yet appeared to be totally unaware that I had been trained in the art of non-contact throughout my entire childhood.

Mum and Dad's roles within the household were clearly defined. Dad went out to work and Mum looked after the home.

Dad was employed by the local Co-operative Society. There was a row of shops in the centre of the village, and Dad spent eleven hours each day earning a living by repairing whatever footwear was brought into the Boot and Shoe Department. During the early years of their marriage, he seemed to be either on piecework — straining to make an adequate wage — or laid off for days at a time when the supply of boots dried up!

Many years later, after he had been promoted to manager of the shop, Mum used to reminisce about the "hard times" when he spent hours pushing me around in my pram because there was no work for him to do. However, one great (and no doubt unexpected) benefit of the job was that shoe repairing was a "reserved" occupation, which meant that when war broke out in 1939, Dad was not called up to fight for King and country. Mum and I did not have the trauma of seeing him posted abroad and facing enemy action. Instead, he was drafted into the Special Police Force, and spent several nights each week patrolling the streets of Littleborough to ensure that law and order were maintained, and that help was at hand should the enemy decide to bomb our peaceful village!

It was the fact that Dad was in the "Specials" that gave our postman, Mr Bateman, the opportunity to tease me. Whenever he saw me, which happened to be almost every day, he would call, "Hello, Policeman!" and then continue merrily on his rounds. I could never make any sense of it at all, and when I asked Dad about it, he would just shake his head and look perplexed.

It is easy to gloss over Dad's single-step promotion to manager of the Co-operative Society Boot and Shoe Department in Littleborough, but it was, in fact, a remarkable achievement. As a cobbler, he used to wear a leather apron and work with a colleague in an upstairs room over the back of the shop. Each day was spent at the bench repairing boots and shoes of all types, using glue (boiled up in a pan), rivets, stitching machines, reamers and a variety of knives and other equipment.

The manager of the shop, Mr Butterworth, had quite a different role. With the help of a female assistant, he had a dressed-up job downstairs, meeting the public and fitting shoes in the men's or ladies' fitting-rooms. He also travelled some fifteen miles by bus every week to the Co-operative Wholesale Society warehouse in Balloon Street, Manchester, to buy stock. The jobs were completely different. The manager wore a suit, Dad wore overalls; the manager used his sales techniques, Dad used his hands.

Even so, on a number of occasions when Mr Butterworth or the shop assistant was ill, Dad had to step into the breach downstairs and serve the public. It turned out that he was both a good salesman and well-liked by customers. So when the time came for Mr Butterworth to retire, the General Manager of the Society, Mr Rigg, came to see my father.

"Arnold," he said, "I've been giving the matter some thought, and I'd like you to take on the manager's job here. Think it over and let me know tomorrow morning."

Mum and Dad must have spent a good deal of time discussing the matter that evening, but the following day when Mr Rigg came to see my father he was in for a surprise. Dad said he wouldn't take the job — he was not sure he was up to it.

Mr Rigg was both surprised and annoyed.

He spoke sternly.

"Arnold Broome, when the General Manager of a Co-operative Society offers you the manager's position in a shop, you don't turn it down. I shall tell the Committee I have found the right man for the post, and you will be appointed when Mr Butterworth retires."

It turned out to be a brilliant appointment. Dad became a very competent manager indeed. He was a shrewd buyer and made many friends through his visits to Balloon Street every Tuesday. Occasionally, a range of footwear would become available at a knock-down price, provided the buyer took the lot. Using his buyer's intuition, Dad would often make the purchase and then

18

sell most of the goods over the next few months. What was left he put in the annual Sale.

I remember one summer he bought dozens of Wellington boots — all sizes — for 2/6d a pair, and during the following hard winter sold most of them for 17/6d. A handsome profit, but the customers were well pleased because in other shops they might well have paid over £1.00.

During the whole time Dad managed the shop, he always made a very good dividend. At the height of its popularity in the 1940s, Littleborough Co-operative Society paid a "divi" of about one shilling, but Dad's shop made around half-a-crown in the pound. As he often said, "If this had been our own shop, Hilda, we'd have made a fortune by now."

Dad's visits to Balloon Street were something of a social occasion as well as an opportunity to buy stock. I remember accompanying him several times during the school holidays and enjoyed going up and down in the huge lifts, and being greeted by the warehousemen who had become Dad's friends.

"Is this your lad, Arnold?"

"Aye, he's come with me today — keeping me in order."

"Is he going to go into the shoe trade?"

"I think he's got more sense!"

But the most memorable part of each trip was the lunch provided for all the visiting buyers. Around noon, Dad and I would make our way down to the vast dining room in the basement of the warehouse. It was set out

19

with long tables covered in white linen cloths, and populated by waitresses wearing black uniforms and white aprons.

Dad would make for a group of his special friends — managers of Shoe Departments from all over the North of England — and for the next hour they would converse about, grumble about and discuss matters Co-operative. The meal, served by waitresses, usually comprised soup with a roll, a main course of meat and two vegetables, followed by sponge pudding and custard.

Although he rarely returned home before 4.00p.m. on what should have been his half-day, I think Dad's visit to Manchester every Tuesday was the highlight of his working week.

Mum's task was to manage the house on whatever money Dad brought home at the end of the week. Although this must have been difficult at times, at least she had the satisfaction of knowing that Dad always "tipped up" the whole of his wage on Friday night.

His own father (Grandad Broome) had been a drinker in his younger days, and seeing his mother taking in washing whilst the old man drank away the family income had had a profound effect upon him. Dad took his role as provider very seriously, and spent little on himself. Throughout my entire childhood I never saw him enter a public house, or involve himself in any form of gambling. His only pleasure was smoking a pipe filled with St Bruno tobacco.

Mum took the role of housewife very seriously too. From the first weeks of their marriage she kept a record in a little notebook of the amount spent on various aspects of running the home. In the year that I was born — 1937 — Dad's weekly wage was around £3. 10s. 0d per week.

During the week beginning July 21st 1939, her accounts read as follows:

July 21/1939

	£	s.	d.
Pearl, Britannic, Oddfellows, Blackburn, R. London		5	0
Rent		8	11½
Order		10	4½
Coal			
Milk		3	3
Papers			10
Bread			11
Meat		3	9
Wakes		5	0
Helliwell's, Speak, Price and Rubies		6	7
Biscuits, toffee		1	0½
Pram	1	2	6
R. socks, A. socks		1	6
Quickies, Dress shields		1	0
Stamps		1	0
	3	11	8½
2suits		3	8
	3	15	4½

£3-10s-0d   5/4½d behind, 12/-d for food
17/4½d in all

The first bills to be paid were the premiums on a number of insurance policies, and then came the basic expenses of lighting, heating and food. The word "Order" refers to goods bought from the local branch of the Co-op Grocery Department, and "Wakes" denotes a holiday fund that was drawn at "Wakes Week" when all the local mills closed for their annual holiday.

The four names that appear together on one line are the names of shopkeepers from whom Mum had a regular weekly order. Mr Speak was a greengrocer who called round at the house every Friday on his bicycle to bring our goods (usually coinciding with my bathtime in front of the fire), and Ruby Jones kept the post office and general store just across the road from us on Laneside.

Of course, items of clothing also had to be bought and both Dad and I were lucky enough to get new pairs of socks that week. I assume that the two suits were for me, but I am not sure what the amount opposite "Pram" refers to. Mum must have found it difficult to manage at times. The accounts above show that, even though the coal merchant had not called that week, she had overspent by a considerable amount. However, on most pages in the notebook a small surplus is shown which Mum put by for a rainy day.

And so my parents became established in their new home, both working hard and taking their responsibilities seriously. I wonder how they felt about rearing the one and only child in the entire family?

CHAPTER
TWO

The Carer and the Boss

As I grew up, I gradually came to recognise that Mum was the Carer and Dad was the Boss, and from my earliest years there was an element of fear in my relationship with him. It's difficult to be certain how this originated, but a clue may lie in my very first memory.

When I was about three I was given a "fairy cycle" as a present — a tiny tricycle with solid rubber tyres and pedals fixed to the front wheel. Apparently, with the aid of this vehicle I strayed away from home one afternoon, although I don't remember any reason for doing so, and was missing for a period of time. I am not sure about the length of my "trip" or where my travels took me, but I do remember clearly the circumstances of my return.

Having been found by the search party, I was brought in at the back door and, standing at the foot of the staircase which led up from the kitchen, I was questioned by Mum and Dad about my absence. Whether I said something which was insolent, or whether I did not show sufficient remorse I do not know, but I have a clear picture of Dad suddenly "exploding" in anger and then chasing me upstairs. He must have banged the treads behind me with the palms of his hands for the noise seemed to follow me until, terrified, I reached the safety of my bedroom.

This seemingly minor incident had a profound effect on me. Of course, I now realise that Dad was play-acting and had never intended to catch me or hurt me, but I do think that the episode affected me in ways that he would never have anticipated. The dose of terror I received from Dad as a result of my "journey of exploration" would undoubtedly have influenced me with regard to future ventures. It would have linked "taking initiative" with "fear" rather than excitement and a sense of adventure. Consequently, I developed as a child who conformed and obeyed, rather than one who challenged and explored.

The pattern was set. Throughout my infancy and childhood, although I can never remember being treated unfairly or severely punished, one stern look from Dad would fill me with instant fear and persuade me to change my behaviour immediately. And I believe it all began with that formational incident involving a fairy cycle.

However, I must not give the impression that life with Dad was a negative experience, for I had many enjoyable times in his company. Soon after he married, Dad had rented a piece of land from the local Cricket Club and, following his family tradition, fenced it off and transformed it into a "hen-pen". In fact, the fencing off was a continuous process as the wooden railings, which had to be high enough to prevent the hens making a break for freedom, were in a semi-permanent state of dilapidation.

During the war, timber was not easy to come by and in any case was very expensive, so all sorts of sources were tapped. I remember on one occasion Dad managed to get hold of some disused beer barrels which he broke open to reclaim the staves. These were, of course, not only curved but tapered at both ends. They were duly put to use and became part of the fence — being perfectly adequate for the purpose, but giving a very odd appearance.

The so-called "hen-pen" was divided into two rectangular areas which were separated by a row of sheds. The front of these sheds opened on to the hen-run itself, which was devoid of grass and muddy in wet weather; to their rear was a larger piece of land which was cultivated to form a garden.

Twice each day throughout the years of my childhood, Dad would walk the three hundred yards to "see to the hens" as he put it. His first visit would be early in the morning before he left for work, the second in the evening, after the evening meal.

"Seeing to the hens" involved topping up their fresh water container and providing them with a trough full of "mash". This was made by chopping up the day's potato peelings and discarded vegetable leaves together with a scoopful of meal. The meal was kept in a bin at the back of one of the sheds and the chopping was done with a home-made chopper made from a length of heavy wood with a T-handle at the top and several parallel blades fixed to the bottom.

The next job was scraping off the dropping board. Under the hens' roosting perch, which they used overnight, was a horizontal board placed there to catch their droppings. This was cleaned using a metal scraper and then sprinkled with lime stored in another tub at the back of the shed.

The final tasks were the most enjoyable — throwing down a handful of corn and walking along the row of nesting boxes collecting the eggs!

During the dark winter months "seeing to the hens" would be completed as speedily as possible, but during the spring and summer I would often accompany Dad on his evening visit and at weekends, and spend hours in the fresh air either helping with the poultry or cultivating the crops.

For me, the former activity was not without its hazards. Dad's stock of Rhode Island Reds and White Leghorns rarely exceeded a dozen but as he was in the habit of breeding his own chicks, he usually kept a cockerel to ensure the eggs were fertile. This succession of cockerels was the bane of my life! Although they differed in ferocity, almost all of them — at one time or another — took exception to my entering the chicken run. As soon as I walked in through the gate, they would fly up at me in true cock-fighting style, flapping their wings and lifting their feet to attack me with their spurs. Usually, I was either forced to retreat or make a dash for the nearest shed.

When Christmas came along though, I got my revenge. In those days, roast chicken was a luxury, and it was only on the twenty-fifth of December that most families could afford such a treat.

A few days before the festive season, Dad and I would set out on our annual mission to catch and prepare our Christmas dinner. Several days previously, Dad would have identified which birds were to be sacrificed — their fate depended on their age, state of health and ability to produce eggs — and one evening, after they had gone to roost, the evil deed was done. Immediately after their necks had been wrung (there were usually two hens involved — one for ourselves and one for Mum's cousin), they were hung by their legs from the roof of the shed and a large tub placed beneath each one. Whilst in this position, still warm and flapping spasmodically, Dad and I began to pluck them, and once this had been completed, they were drawn and taken home to Mum.

I am aware that this process sounds utterly barbaric, but as a child I accepted it without a hint of guilt or squeamishness. It has to be remembered that in those days meat did not come into the home on a plastic tray sealed under a transparent covering. It was wrapped in white paper by the family butcher who had cut it up on his wooden block before one's very eyes. So killing and dressing a chicken did not seem in any way out of the ordinary.

Whilst on the subject of food, most of what I ate as a child was very plain and simple. Many of the items would turn the stomachs of people nowadays. Slices of bread spread with beef dripping, tripe of various kinds, pig's trotters, cow-heel and mussels all formed a regular part of our varied but primitive diet. Occasionally, even more bizarre delicacies would be enjoyed. Grandad Broome and Dad occasionally tucked into sheep's brains, whilst Auntie Nellie's speciality was a stew containing beef, tripe and cow-heel, the latter providing gelatine (which acted as a thickener) and a number of porous bones from which the "juice" could be sucked to increase one's enjoyment!

However, there was one "pre-packed" food which, because of the hen-pen, was enjoyed regularly by our family — the egg! They were sometimes large, sometimes small, occasionally double-yolked, but always nutritious. At a time when eggs were rationed, we were fortunate always to have as many as we needed. And we were able to supply our friends and neighbours, too.

The other half of the hen-pen was taken up by the garden. Dad grew a range of vegetables such as potatoes, onions, beetroot, cabbages, peas, and salad crops. He also managed to get a good yield from his tomato plants, which he grew in a small, unheated greenhouse in the middle of the plot.

Although I pottered around the garden area, I never really helped in the production of vegetables. My main activities were picking and eating the peas before they got anywhere near the pan, and fertilising the tomato flowers with a rabbit's tail tied to a cane. Not that I didn't receive encouragement. Dad marked out a couple of square yards in a fairly unproductive part of the garden and allowed me to try to cultivate it. But as there were no child-sized tools and the land was fairly hard and stony, most of the seeds I put into the soil never came up.

In spite of this failure, I look back on my days at the hen-pen with pleasure. The combination of fresh air and open space provided an environment in which I could explore, experiment and work off my surplus energy. Here began my enjoyment of the countryside, love of nature and interest in gardening.

Dad was usually busy with one task or another and I had all the freedom I desired. Rarely whilst I was at the hen-pen did I receive a "stern look". Indeed, the only time I *did* get into trouble, Dad colluded in the process.

One afternoon, when I was about five, I invited a friend to accompany me to the hen-pen. It was a very hot day in summer and Dad had decided to tar the roofs of the sheds. This job, which he did periodically, involved spreading pitch over the roofing felt with an old hand brush. On this occasion, Dad must either have been distracted for some reason, or had a mental aberration, because during the course of the afternoon — with his full permission — my pal and I found ourselves on top of the largest shed with a bucket of tar, wielding a couple of brushes!

By the time he came to his senses, we had managed to get tar all over ourselves. I don't know what happened to my friend when he was taken home by one of my embarrassed parents, but I do know that it took many applications of butter (still on ration!) before I was free from pitch.

★ ★ ★

When I was not helping Dad at the hen-pen, I would play on Laneside with my friends. Calderbrook Road was very quiet in those days, the main traffic being horse-drawn vehicles and the occasional slow-moving car, so Mum had no qualms about allowing me to play on the footpath, or even at the edge of the road. I had three friends as a small child. Gerald Pickering lived about a hundred yards away, close to the allotments, and his next-door-but-one neighbour was Peter Garlick. Gerald actually shared my birthday and Peter was a few weeks younger. Gwen Kershaw, who was of a similar age, was also allowed to play with us, even though she was a girl!

Many of our games seemed to be played in the gutter at the side of the road, and rotated with the seasons. In summer, when it was hot, one of our favourites was "marbles". I know there are many versions of the game but ours must have been the simplest — two of us would merely take it in turns to roll our "alley" along the gutter and try to hit the marble owned by our friend. When we did so, we claimed it as our own and promptly put it into our bag.

Well, that was the theory, but in fact there were a whole range of unwritten rules which came into play as the game progressed. To begin with, having struck and therefore won a marble, one was often prevented from keeping it because one had not said the word "Keepers" before the game started. And what is more, if the marble was a "blood-alley" (streaked with red and white), one had to hit it *twice* in order to own it. The same rule applied to "dobbers", extra large marbles which were highly prized. These rules, along with frequent disputes as to whether a marble had, or had not, been hit quite often led to a game ending in a long cross argument, with members of the gang taking sides.

By the time we had tired of marbles, the "jacks" season had arrived. A set of jacks consisted of five small wooden cubes (about the size of a sugar-lump), and a glass or clay marble. The idea was to throw the marble into the air and whilst it was airborne, pick up a jack with the same hand and then catch it again. Having picked up all five in this way, one would throw them down again and progress to "twoses", now picking up two at a time. This was followed by "threeses", "fourses", and "fiveses". The game then became more and more demanding, as claps or other actions were inserted between the throws. Any failure, such as dropping the marble, or picking up the wrong number of jacks, marked the end of one's turn and the jacks were handed to one's opponent. Quite often when the "jacks" season arrived, we did not have the authentic equipment, but improvised for a while with a marble and five small pebbles until we could afford to buy a proper set from the newsagent's shop on Hare Hill Road in Littleborough.

Another favourite summer game was "whip and top". A long piece of string was attached to a cane or stick and the bullet-shaped spinning top, which was decorated with circles of chalk, was set spinning on the footpath. The pavements along Calderbrook Road were made out of slabs of smooth stone, so as long as one avoided the cracks between them one could keep it going for ages. Competitions were sometimes held to see which top would remain upright the longest, and once again arguments broke out about why various failures had occurred.

A more exciting version of "whip and top" could be played if one or more of the group had a "window-breaker". This was a top shaped more or less like a mushroom, which flew through the air when whipped. With a little practice, most of us could transform this type of top into a dangerous missile, causing it to zoom several yards at head height before finally landing — still spinning — ten yards away. It was easy to understand why they were called "window-breakers", but I cannot remember a pane of glass ever being shattered by one.

A rather more active pastime, and one that frequently got us into trouble, was inspired by the Saturday afternoon films at the local cinema! All through the summer months the field next to my house was populated by a herd of cows. These belonged to the Easterby family, whose farmhouse was further along Calderbrook Road. Mr and Mrs Easterby were already old when I was a child, but were helped by their son, Eric, who did the daily milk run on the horse-drawn float, and carried out a lot of work on the farm. Occasionally, when we had tired of the more conventional games, we would decide to play at "cowboys and Indians" — and this, of course, involved rounding up cows.

Very often, as we were galloping across the field on imaginary horses, slapping our hips with our right hands to urge ourselves on, and scattering the animals in all directions, an irate figure would appear from the farmyard in the distance. Accompanied by a sheepdog and wielding a long stick, Eric would hurry towards us shouting, "I'll give thee t'boot, I'll give thee t'boot!" And we, sensing the danger, would turn our trusty steeds towards the edge of the field and immediately disappear in the opposite direction! Considering how often this happened, I am surprised that Eric did not complain to our parents, but I don't remember him ever doing so.

When Spring came along our thoughts turned to frog-spawn and tadpoles. Running alongside Dad's hen-pen was a little brook which sometimes had frog-spawn in it, but much better sources were the ponds and lodges which were often found alongside the local cotton mills. When we had gone through the complicated procedure of tying a piece of string around the neck of a jam jar to form a handle, we were fully equipped, for none of us had a fishing net. Looking back now, this frog-spawn gathering was a highly dangerous occupation and indeed, every couple of years or so some poor child would be found floating face down in one of the lodges, but this did not seem to deter us nor cause our parents to forbid the activity.

Once the spawn had hatched, I would check every day to see how the tadpoles were developing. One very successful year, they actually grew big enough to grow back legs — but to my great disappointment I never succeeded in rearing a frog.

Autumn brought with it the conker season and a whole new round of activity. First, one had to acquire a conker, either by finding a horse-chestnut tree in the neighbourhood or cadging one from another child who had managed to get a supply. Then, after boring a hole through the centre of it (usually with a skewer), one had to make it HARD. There were a great many ways of achieving this, most of which I tried and none of which seemed to work very well. The most common method was to soak the conker overnight in vinegar and place it in a warm oven.

Finally, having done the best one could, the time came to test it in combat. My conkers used to stay intact for a couple of contests at the most, but there were always some boys who would proudly take a brown, wizened horse chestnut from their pocket and, holding it up by the string for everyone to admire, declare that it was a "Sevener" or even a "Fifteener". There was never any proof of course.

As we grew a little older, perhaps eight or nine, we began to take a delight in "playing tricks". These were relatively harmless, but seemed to give us a great deal of pleasure. The most common escapade was "knocking at doors and running away", but as the simple version soon palled, we thought up a more sophisticated variation. Having tied together the doorknobs of two adjacent houses in a row with a long piece of cord, we would knock simultaneously on both doors and retire to watch the fun. As the first householder tried to open his door, he would find he was impeded, but when the second occupier did the same, the door of the first house would slam shut.

This caused us no end of amusement, but it was very expensive in terms of string, which had to be acquired from home when our parents were otherwise occupied. Local people must have known who the culprits were, but I don't think they ever complained. They all seemed to take it in good part.

There were, however, two occasions when our behaviour did bring trouble down upon us. On the first occasion, we had wandered up Calderbrook Road until we reached Clough Road, a well-made track that led up into the hills. I knew the area well because along this road was Greenhill Methodist Chapel, where Mum and Dad had been married and where I attended Sunday school every week.

Just beyond the chapel stood the ruins of an old mill and a cluster of houses, and close by were a number of sheds and a few hen-pens. As we roved around the area, we came upon a pile of house bricks stacked neatly along a window ledge of the ruined mill and, finding a large circular pit nearby (which had probably been a dyeing vat), we all began to throw in the bricks with enthusiasm.

Imagine our reaction when, as the last few bricks descended into the hole, a man suddenly emerged from one of the hen-pens and approached us in a furious temper. Apparently, he was the owner of the bricks and had intended to use them on some project or other, and as we had now disposed of them, he told us that we had to pay for them! In spite of our protestations that we did not realise the bricks were valuable (which was true) and profuse apologies, the man insisted on writing down our names and addresses in a book, and we all went home to break the terrible news to our parents.

Two days later, Sergeant Whitehead of the Littleborough Police Force knocked on our door and was invited in by my father. Looking back now, I think it is likely that he and my father colluded in deciding to give me a shock — and in that they certainly succeeded. By the time the policeman had left, I was very subdued and had agreed to pay back the cost of the bricks from my weekly "spends". In reality, I learned later that my father — and possibly the other parents — had recompensed the man for his loss.

Our second escapade was most unsavoury and concerned tub toilets! A tub-toilet building had a unique design. At the front was a wooden door through which users entered, and inside, fixed across the cubicle some two feet from the floor, was a flat wooden platform containing a large circular hole with smoothed edges. Beneath this seat was placed a metal tub, shaped like half a barrel, and access to this was gained from the back of the building through a low door rather like the bottom half of a stable door.

It did not take us long, as children, to realise that if we crept up to the rear of one of these buildings when it was occupied and quietly opened the rear door, some very interesting sights would meet our eyes.

Close to Dad's hen-pen was a block of three tub-toilets and suffice to say that one day, as "the gang" were lurking in readiness at the rear of the building, we were discovered by one of our potential victims and reported to our parents. Although I escaped a good hiding, I was subjected to a long lecture and spent the rest of the day in bed!

One thing which I must mention when talking about "our gang", is the arrival of a new child in the neighbourhood — and how he was excluded from the group.

When we were around six or seven years old, Neville Thompson came to live next door to Gwen Kershaw. Somehow or other, in our childish way, we immediately identified him as "scruffy" and would have nothing to do with him. It may have been because on a number of occasions the school nurse had found he had head-lice, or perhaps it was because he came from what in those days was called "a broken home" (one-parent families hadn't been invented). Whatever the reason, we were unwilling to allow him to join our group.

He must have been very unhappy at times, for not only did we refuse to play with him, we also gave him the nickname of "Nitty Neville". Without doubt, children can be very cruel at times.

My relationship with Mum did not contain the element of fear which marked my relationship with Dad, but neither did it contain any great closeness or companionship. I have no recollections of Mum playing games with me, although I feel sure she must have done so from time to time.

As I have said, I do not think Mum was naturally a warm person, but throughout my childhood, she displayed a selfless attitude towards caring for me which she equated with love. In short, she expressed her devotion to me through dedication. The single episode which best exemplifies this attitude can be illustrated by what happened when an epidemic of scarlet fever broke out in our neighbourhood when I was five or six years old.

For several weeks the ambulance had been travelling back and forth along Calderbrook Road, taking the latest victim of the disease to the "Fever Hospital" some six miles away. There was an atmosphere both at school and in the neighbourhood of, "I wonder who will be next?" The victims were invariably children and horrific pictures were painted in the tales which passed from child to child about what happened when you were taken away in the "Fever Wagon"!

Although I was not aware of it at the time, Mum had a mortal fear of hospitals that had possibly arisen from a serious illness during her teenage years, and she decided that under no circumstances was I going to be taken away and admitted to such an institution. This fear transferred itself to me, because I too dreaded the thought of going into hospital and have vague memories of expressing my feelings tearfully at this time.

However, the infection had no favourites and when eventually I began to display the dreaded symptoms, the doctor came and confirmed that I had the illness. I do not know what negotiations took place between my parents and the local G.P., but persuading him to allow me to stay at home could not have been easy. Many of our neighbours' children had already been taken away, and it must have been difficult for Mum to insist that the same fate was not going to happen to me.

When the doctor eventually gave in and agreed to my staying at home, it was on the understanding that certain conditions were fulfilled. First, during the anticipated six-week period of illness, Dad had to move out of the house and not re-enter until he was given the all-clear. Second, Mum had to remain alone in the house with me and not leave the premises until I was fully recovered. Third, at the end of the isolation period, a fumigation team had to come to the house and spray the walls, floors, furniture, clothes and all personal effects.

Amazingly, this is in fact what happened! Dad packed his suitcase and went to stay at Grandma Broome's house. He came to the house daily with a supply of food, which he left on the doorstep for Mum to collect. All messages were shouted through the letterbox and when, after a couple of weeks, I was allowed to leave my sick-bed and go downstairs, Dad would often appear at the front window with my grandparents or a couple of aunts, who would mime in an animated way through the glass.

Mum was confined to the house for the whole six weeks, nursing me for the initial two weeks and then "feeding me up" on calves-foot jelly when I was convalescing.

I have often wondered what the neighbours made of it all, and whether my parents were ridiculed or admired. It certainly must have been strange to see a group of relatives encircling our front window, waving and calling out messages to the two inmates.

Finally, when I had fully recovered, but before any of my family or other visitors were allowed into the house, two men wearing special clothing arrived and proceeded to spray some sort of vapour over everything. I remember Mum recounting on several occasions how they had put all the books I had been reading into a pile, and then gone through them page by page, fumigating each one!

Mum's self-sacrificing approach to life should not be undervalued. She did indeed give up a great deal at times to do what she thought was right, or show care to others. Being more religious than Dad, self-denial fitted in well with her concept of Christianity, and there is no doubt that lots of people benefited. Occasionally, however, a hint of self-righteousness could be detected alongside her self-sacrifice. Many years later, she told me with some pride that I had been breast-fed until I was nine months old (the implication being that this was dedication beyond the call of duty), and The Saga of Christmas Eve was repeated from time to time to emphasise her true altruism in the face of adversity.

The Saga of Christmas Eve was not confined to my childhood years but was told and retold by Mum throughout her life. It described how, although weary as a result of working until 7.00p.m. on the day before Christmas, every year she and Dad had to hurry home in order to attend the family party which was held at Grandma Broome's. Then, having walked home in the early hours of Christmas morning and put me to bed, they were faced with preparing for their own family party on Christmas Day.

She was indignant that everyone in the family *insisted* it should be held at our house, because they wanted to see how I, as the only child in the family, enjoyed playing with my Christmas toys. No-one seemed to realise, she complained, that she and Dad were exhausted. They didn't understand what it was like to work *and* bring up a family.

Nevertheless, Mum always soldiered on without revealing her true feelings and never let them know they were imposing on her. I suppose it didn't occur to her that most of the toys I had received had been given to me by the "thoughtless relatives" she grumbled about.

I should not leave Mum without mentioning that she had a fine soprano singing voice, and that prior to her marriage she was often booked as a soloist to sing at church services and concerts in and around Littleborough. Her talent must have been recognised early — possibly at Greenhill Chapel — because during her teenage years she took lessons with Welcome Mitchell, a highly respected local singing teacher who had links with the Chapel.

I still have a letter in my possession dated 30th October 1928 and addressed: *"Dear Miss Ackroyd"* in which she is invited to sing at Bottoms Primitive Methodist Church on Saturday 24th November. It is obvious that her ability was recognised, as one sentence in the letter is somewhat apologetic:

"Now as to terms, I am sorry I cannot offer anything great, just expenses, say 5/-."

Compared with Dad's weekly wage of £3.10s.0d for around 48 hours' work ten years later, this is not as poor an offer as it may appear!

As a child, I remember hearing Mum sing occasionally in the house, and *very* occasionally she would sing at a family party, but as far as I know she never sang in a concert after I was born. One of her favourites was "In My Sweet Little Alice Blue Gown", and I can still hear her voice whenever I think of this tune. So perhaps Mum made her greatest sacrifice when she gave up a potentially profitable singing career in order to marry Dad and start a family. I hope she never regretted it.

CHAPTER
THREE

High Days and Holidays

My earliest memories of school are happy ones. The "baby class" at Littleborough Central Board School into which I was admitted at the age of five was under the care of a teacher called Miss Whip who, fortunately for all concerned, lived up to her name in appearance only — not in behaviour. Being tall and slim, with a very wrinkled face, she seemed to my childish eyes to be as old as Methuselah, but she had quiet ways and a kind attitude which made the children in her care feel happy and secure.

The classroom in which we spent our days had part-tiled walls, tall narrow windows and a polished wooden floor. In the centre of one wall, surrounded by a metal fire-guard, was an open coal fire, and my clearest memories are of sitting in a group around this fire, drinking milk through a straw from one of the small bottles which had been warming on the hearth all morning.

On the opposite side of the classroom stood a tall, grey rocking horse who rewarded each industrious or helpful pupil in the class with a ride on his back. And there could be no cheating in this regard, as all of us found it impossible to mount "Dobbin" without the help of Miss Whip! However, even though many children earned this treat, when it came to sitting in Dobbin's leather saddle some five feet from the floor and being rocked back and forth by the teacher, several of them found it to be a frightening experience. So it is true to say that the old horse caused as many tears as smiles.

I remember little of any schoolwork we did in the "baby class", so I must have found it either enjoyable, or at least non-threatening. However, I do have one clear picture of Miss Whip sitting before the blazing fire one afternoon with long metal tubes — which I have since realised were cigar containers — pushed on to her fingers. The class was engaged in some form of counting practice, because she asked each of us in turn to remove one of the tubes and call out the appropriate number as we did so. When it came to *my* turn, I found it took a remarkable amount of strength to pull off the tube! Apart from this one incident my first year of full-time education is a complete blur.

In Class Two, my main recollection is of Miss Butterworth, the pretty young schoolmistress with honey blonde hair who was our teacher. All the boys in the class were in love with her and one day after school, a friend and I decided to stay behind in the hope of being allowed to give her a kiss. I can still remember the thrill we experienced when our wish was granted.

The Mistress in charge of Class Three was a well-organised teacher. Each morning as we entered the classroom, we were greeted by the sight of several rows of sums which she had already chalked up on the blackboard. As my arithmetic was extremely shaky, my heart used to sink at the prospect of working through all the columns — and I was often one of the last to finish. However, I made up for this deficiency by being reasonably competent at reading and spelling, and thus managed to survive *her* educational programme without too much difficulty.

And so my early years in the Infant Department passed uneventfully. Although I cannot say I enjoyed going to school, initially, it was not an upsetting or distressing experience either.

Of course, as these were the "war years", one regular occurrence with which we had to cope was "Air Raid Practice". Every now and then the air raid siren on the roof of the Council Offices in Hare Hill Park would be sounded, and immediately we would put down our pencils or crayons and line up at the classroom door. Then, following our teacher in single file, we would cross the yard to one of the brick and concrete shelters that had been erected around the perimeter of the school playground. After the register had been called, we lined up once more and returned to the classroom to resume lessons.

I do not remember anyone being frightened or upset by this procedure. We accepted it as a normal part of school life, in much the same way that we accepted plimsolls were required for P.T. and milk was supplied at morning playtime.

At home, all our parents had been issued with gas masks for their own use and, years later, I remember Mum telling me about a sort of "incubator box" which had been provided for me as a baby. Apparently, at the wail of the siren, I would be placed inside this contraption and the whole family would descend to the coal cellar!

Although I cannot recall this "box", one thing I *do* remember as a very small child was owning a Mickey Mouse gas mask with a valve on the front through which I could blow a raspberry as I breathed out. But I had no comprehension that it had anything to do with counteracting danger.

School holidays came around frequently, and many of them seemed to contain a festival or event to celebrate. Christmas, for example, was the "party season". I have already mentioned Grandma Broome's party held on Christmas Eve, followed by my parents' party on Christmas Day, but this was by no means the end of the celebrations. A week later, on New Year's Eve, it was Charlie and Ethel's turn to host yet another party.

The same family members attended each of these gatherings and they all followed a similar pattern. As the guests arrived, their coats were taken upstairs and laid across a bed, as there was no way they could be accommodated downstairs. Then everyone would crowd into the front room where every chair in the house had been arranged in a large circle. Conversation or games followed until, during the early evening, a buffet was served in the kitchen. This was simple fare compared with today. No vol-au-vents, pâté or pasta twirls, but small pork pies, plates of sliced chicken, ham and ox tongue. Alongside these would be two glass bowls — one containing sage and onion stuffing and the other apple sauce. There was also a dish of onion rings and sliced cucumber soaked in vinegar, some sticks of celery in a jug and a huge plate of bread and butter. For dessert there was sherry trifle, some bowls of tinned fruit and a jug of Carnation evaporated milk.

The cakes were home-made, including the Christmas cake which took pride of place in the centre of the table; it was usually decorated with some sprigs of holly and a number of little pottery or plaster figures. Across the rippled icing Father Christmas could be seen speeding on his sleigh towards a red-roofed cottage, or two warmly wrapped children would be found standing by a minute Christmas tree admiring a snowman.

In addition to all this, here and there around the house were bowls of sweets, nuts and crisps which one could eat whenever one wished! One item that only ever seemed to appear at Christmas was "Twiglets". These were savoury snacks shaped like wobbly drinking straws and covered with little buds of brown material that tasted of Marmite. Several of my relatives found these to be very "moreish", and I was almost addicted to them!

Occasionally, a new person would turn up at one of these parties — perhaps a friend of one of my aunts — and usually they became the victim of a good-humoured (if somewhat sadistic) practical joke. Two

47

such jokes spring to mind. The first involved inaugurating the guest into the "Mustard Club". Following a long, complicated procedure in which the newcomer was seated on a chair, blindfolded, and asked to repeat a solemn pledge, a large teaspoonful of English mustard was spooned into his mouth. Of course, this caused no end of eye-watering discomfort for the victim, and no end of amusement for everyone else.

The second practical joke had a lavatorial theme. The victim was asked to sit on a chair before a baking bowl filled with water. At the bottom of it was a silver coin — perhaps a sixpence or a shilling — and the candidate was asked to memorise its position. The hapless individual was then blindfolded and told that if he could remove the coin with one single hand movement, he could keep the coin. The moment the blindfold was in position a chamber pot was substituted for the baking bowl. This had been half-filled with water — coloured with gravy browning — and several fingers of bread had been floated in it. Imagine the shock and dismay when, feeling around for the coin, the victim's blindfold was suddenly removed and he saw the container in which his hand was placed!

Gales of laughter would rock the room and later, as the victim related his feelings to the group, further roars of laughter followed. It was what in later years was called "making your own fun"!

However, there was one aspect of Ethel and Charlie's party, which, as a small child, filled me with dread. As I have said, it was held on New Year's Eve, and this was the evening when "mummers" toured the district. With blackened faces and armed with brooms, groups of young people would move from house to house sweeping away the Old Year in preparation for the New. The tradition was that they did not knock to gain admittance, but walked straight into one's living room, humming loudly and refusing to leave until their palms were crossed with silver.

The fact is that I never actually saw a mummer, but the adults' graphic descriptions of them, combined with my own vivid imagination, made me terrified at the thought of them. So much so, that Auntie Ethel kept the outside doors locked throughout the entire evening.

As Easter approached, acting began to occupy my mind. The "Pace Egg Play" is a traditional play that has been performed in the North of England at Easter time for centuries. Its history is not clear, but it is reminiscent of the well-known Mystery Plays. It is thought that the word "pace" may be a corruption of the word "peace" and the story is of good overcoming evil.

In the past, adults acted it out in market squares, but all I knew as a child was that on Good Friday morning gangs of local children went around the streets giving performances in the middle of the road, and taking a collection from householders who came out to watch. Gerald, Peter, Gwen and myself, along with Ian, Gerald's younger brother who was roped in to help, laid claim to Laneside and the lower part of

Calderbrook Road as our territory. Other gangs earmarked localities close to their homes.

Our first task was to allocate parts, and this was done amidst many arguments. The number of characters was dependent on the actors available, so of course we had five — St George, St Andrew, the Doctor, Beelzebub and Slasher. Then each of us set about making our costumes, including shields, swords, helmets and other props.

Once school had closed for the holidays, rehearsals began in earnest. The traditional words were handed down orally — I never saw them written down — but even now I still remember a few lines:

"I am a brave and noble knight and Slasher is my name . . .

. . . be you alive or be you dead, I'll grind your bones to make my bread."

When Good Friday dawned, all of us were up with the larks. By nine o'clock we had been safety-pinned into our costumes and begun to give our first self-conscious presentation in the middle of Calderbrook Road. The whole drama lasted for about three or four minutes and, at its conclusion, Beelzebub (with blackened face) would go around the crowds of people standing at their front doors and rattle his tin! After that, there was no stopping us — our confidence grew with each repetition.

By tradition, all performances stopped at noon, and the collecting box was opened and our spoils shared. Two hours later, accompanied by our parents, we would be making our way, along with several hundred other people, towards Hollingworth Lake, a local beauty spot. Every year at Easter a travelling fair set up on the Lake Bank car park, and many families in the area headed for the bright lights and music to spend a happy couple of hours testing out the rides or partaking of the candy floss.

On arrival, we would have to fight our way through the masses of people packed around the stalls and rides to get close to the action. Having done so, we would battle to get on the Cyclone, queue to board the ghost train and race across the rink at the end of each session to occupy a Dodgem Car. Eventually, having spent all our money, we would retire from the fray, tired but happy. At the end of the afternoon, with empty pockets, but a smile on our faces, we would return home after a successful day out.

May Day brought with it dancing round the Maypole, but during *my* childhood this was done in the school playground only. I never remember it taking place in the street, although I know that used to happen in the past.

What I do remember about May Day is the decorating of the shire horses by all the companies who kept them. The Co-op Coal Department housed their animals in stables just behind Dad's shop, and the coal men would arrive particularly early on the day in

51

question and make a terrific job of platting ribbons into the horses' manes and tails, polishing their harnesses and hanging brasses along their sides.

Most other carters did the same. The milkmen and the draymen must have been very late home that night as they seemed to spend most of the day sitting proudly on their carts whilst members of the public made admiring comments and patted their horses' noses.

Whitsuntide was when I "walked with the scholars". From a young age, I was sent to Greenhill Primitive Methodist Sunday School twice every Sunday — morning at 10.30 a.m., afternoon at 2.30 p.m. — so like many of my contemporaries I walked in the procession of witness each year.

Mum and I would arrive at the chapel on Whit Friday afternoon (Dad never took part in this) to find that the huge embroidered flag, with its two supporting poles and stout coloured ropes, had been removed from storage and was leaning against the chapel wall. In the kitchen, rows of wicker hand-baskets had been filled with flowers, watered and placed along a surface. Outside the chapel door, clustered together in a haze of cigarette smoke, members of the brass band who were due to accompany us down Calderbrook Road were nervously fingering the valves on their instruments.

Eventually, after what seemed like an age, things would get moving. The baskets of flowers were given out to young girls, proudly wearing new dresses bought for the occasion. The flag was raised by two sturdy men, who placed the poles into sockets hung on leather straps around their necks. The rest of us formed a long column in the road and, as the band struck up, we began to walk in procession towards Hare Hill Park watched by crowds of onlookers.

After the united service around the bandstand, we retraced our steps and spent the rest of the afternoon on the "Whit Friday Field" next to the chapel. There were games to play, races to take part in and refreshments to be enjoyed. It was one of those occasions when it could be said that "a good time was had by all".

When Summer arrived, with its long warm evenings, I would often be taken on family walks around the neighbourhood. Mum's favourite was a sedate stroll along the meandering "carriage drive" of Town House, one of the oldest and largest houses in the district, which was set in its own grounds not far from where we lived. When I was a boy it was owned by the Harvey Family, who were rich mill-owners, and as we walked past it I stared in wonder at its imposing stone frontage, numerous windows and large well-kept gardens.

A longer walk involved a climb up Shore Road, which ran at right angles to Calderbrook Road. As the hill levelled out at the top, one came upon Shore Mills, owned by Sir Cuthbert Clegg, and just beyond this were Shore Gardens, a patchwork of sloping fields full of growing rhubarb surrounded by hawthorn hedges. One of the great advantages of taking the path which wound down between them was that it eventually led to Stubley Brow, and a visit to Grandma Broome's house.

However, from the "top of Shore" (as we called it), three other walks were also available. One could set out along the path through the rhubarb fields, but then make a detour towards Starring Potteries, where piles of brown, earthenware pipes were stacked ready for sale. This route also led towards Grandad Broome's hen-pen, and as we approached it we often saw a tell-tale plume of tobacco smoke rising from amongst his sheds indicating that he was in residence there!

One could also take a bridle path to Wardle Village, which took one past the "Cottage Homes" — a number of large detached houses which had been built, so I was told, to accommodate poor children who had no parents. Or one could turn sharp right, past the William IV Inn and follow the ascending track in front of the ancient Shore Hall and onward to Watergrove.

Watergrove had been a hamlet in the hills above Wardle Village until, in 1935, the people who made up the small community were told to leave their homes as the valley was to be flooded to form a reservoir. By the time I was born, the dam was in place and every sign of habitation had been submerged under a huge expanse of water.

Dad used to tell me that when he was a boy, his Uncle Bob kept a farm at Watergrove, and occasionally he had cows that needed driving to Rochdale Market some four miles away. Dad would get up very early on the day in question and walk to Watergrove to help drive the cattle, returning on foot with Uncle Bob after the animals had been sold. The story always ended in the same way: "A whole day's work and at the end of it he'd give me sixpence!" Dad's wry smile gave away what he thought of his uncle's generosity.

Bonfire Night was very much a family affair whilst I was young. Prior to the big night, my aunties would buy me several boxes of Standard fireworks, and half the fun was taking them out of the box in the days leading up to November 5th and laying them in rows or groups on the table and studying them. Some had names to inspire, like "Volcanic Eruption" or "Death Bomb"; others seemed disappointing even before they were lit, like "Golden Rain" or "Silver Fountain". Several types, which were available then, do not appear to be on sale any longer. Rip-raps — or "jumping-jacks" as I used to call them — came in various lengths, and one could count the bangs by noting the number of folds in the brown paper concertina. In a similar way, the diameter of a catherine wheel gave an indication of how long it would spin.

When it came to Bonfire Night itself, Mum and Dad were definitely in charge. Sometimes we had a very small fire on the little piece of spare ground behind our row of five houses, and at other times there was no fire at all, but merely a firework display. A few toddlers who lived locally were brought along, because it was "safe", and in general the night went off well. To eat, we had potatoes roasted in the fire (usually encased in half an inch of charcoal), treacle toffee and home-made parkin.

The first snow of the Winter brought with it a great desire to own a sledge. There were two places close to home where children went to sledge. The "nursery slope" was in Easterby's field (now empty of cows) right next to my house, where there was a very gentle gradient down to the road. A more demanding run was in Hare Hill Park where the lawn above the bandstand was at a much steeper angle.

But with regard to sledging I had a problem. For a year or two I didn't have a sledge at all (there were no plastic ones on sale!), and when I finally persuaded Dad to make one for me it had a major fault — he did not fit it with metal runners. So even though it was well constructed, it never really worked properly. Whilst others flew down the icy slopes without effort, I could only manage a stately pace and had to assist my progress by pushing with my feet.

During the winter of 1947, when I was just nine years old, we had the heaviest snowfall in living memory. On waking one morning, I thought my attic bedroom seemed dark, and glancing up at the skylight above my head, realised that it was covered with a thick layer of snow. I ran to the gable window and looked out along the length of Calderbrook Road. An amazing sight met my eyes. All the houses and trees on Laneside were merely rounded mounds of whiteness, and the walls surrounding Easterby's field — and the road itself — had completely disappeared. A line of four-foot high lampposts marked the position where it *should* have been but that was all.

Nobody set off to work or school on time that morning. On opening our front door we were faced with a three-foot bank of drifted snow which had to be cleared to reach the roadway, but when we opened the back door to go to the toilet, the snow was above door-level. Dad and I spent most of the morning digging a tunnel to the shared toilet, and indeed for a couple of days until the roof fell in, that is what it was — a white translucent covered pathway through which we walked to the outside lavatory.

When, a day or two later, Dad took me higher up Calderbrook Road, we came to several places where the glass domes of the lampposts were level with my face, and the entire fronts of some houses were still encased in snow, with tunnels cut through to their front doors. It took several days of continuous work by the snowplough to clear the main roads through the village, and the Hebble bus, which journeyed over the nearby Pennines, was out of service for a week or more.

When the long thaw set in we experienced more difficulties, as we had to wade through deep slush whenever we went out. I remember one morning looking through the window at the row of houses opposite and noticing a thick layer of snow which had slid down the roof, hanging like a curtain in front of their upstairs windows. As I watched, the owner of one of the houses walked up and went inside, slamming his front door as he did so, and immediately a "waterfall" of snow cascaded down, creating a huge white pile where, seconds before, the man had been standing. The look of shock on his face when he re-opened the door and saw what had happened remains with me still.

★ ★ ★

And so the year went round. Event followed event and season followed season until Christmas with its parties appeared on the horizon once more.

Although many of my relatives must have experienced anxieties and shortages caused by the war, I do not remember any of their difficulties or deprivations rubbing off on me. As an infant growing up between the years of 1939 and 1945, my educational and social development seemed unaffected. I always felt wanted and important, and had no comprehension of the traumas being experienced by other families as they were bombed out of their homes in nearby cities, or the heartache and fear experienced by those left at home whilst their loved ones fought overseas.

However, my family circumstances were about to change. As I approached the age of seven, and the war was coming to its end, Mum and Dad suggested I might like to have a baby brother or sister. Apparently, I took to this suggestion immediately and, having been informed that Nurse Ellis, the local midwife, brought babies in her black bag, I visited her house one day to make a request for a delivery to Calderbrook Road.

Although I did not realise it at the time, the arrival of this new baby would cause significant changes in my young life.

CHAPTER
FOUR

Sharing the Limelight

Much amusement was caused throughout the family when I went to Nurse Ellis's house to order a baby for Mum and Dad. I remember knocking on the white front door of the stone cottage in Church Street, and making my request to the short, plump woman that opened it. In fact, I ordered two babies at the time — one for Mum and one for Auntie Ethel — but only one was ever delivered.

It seems strange now, in these days of enlightenment, that a six-year-old should have had no idea that babies grew inside their mothers. But as far as I was concerned they were delivered by the nurse, and the way to get one was to order one! Nurse Ellis, who no doubt had Mum on her list of expectant mothers at the time, assured me she would do her best to fulfil my request, and I returned home a happy little boy.

It is obvious to me now that Mum and Dad must have primed me in my desire to have a little brother or sister. When they were sure that there was to be an addition to the family, they "put the thought into my head".

Surprisingly, I seem to have taken to the idea. I use the word "surprisingly" because during the early years of the war when I was still a baby, Mum and Dad had been asked to take an evacuee from central Manchester who, according to reports, used to bully me. Years later, Mum told me that during his stay with us the boy's parents had visited him only once, and it was obvious from his behaviour and his clothing that he had been neglected at home. When he arrived, he had had "nits" which he had subsequently passed on to me.

However, in spite of this bad experience, I remember looking forward to the new baby. One day, on returning home from school and finding a pram in the living room, I realised that its arrival must be imminent. Even so, I certainly didn't expect it to be delivered in the middle of the night; so when, a day or two later, I was awakened in the early hours of the morning by a gurgling sound issuing from Mum and Dad's bedroom, there was no thought of a baby in my mind. Lying in the semi-darkness for what seemed like hours, I became convinced that my parents had bought a turkey and for some strange reason had taken it into their room!

Then, much later, when Dad came in to collect me, the mystery was solved. For when he took me in to Mum, she was sitting up in bed holding the cause of all the noise — my baby sister! Whether, as I have always believed, it was really I who chose a name for her, or whether it was my parents who once again "put an idea into my head" I do not know. But it was decided that the new baby was to be called "Maureen".

Who can tell what goes on in the mind of a child when it suddenly finds itself usurped from its central position in a family? When, instead of being "Number

One" — the focus of all attention — it discovers that it has to share the limelight with a new arrival. Many children have to live through such an experience and most manage to survive it without too much upset.

In my case, I do not think I very coped well with the arrival of the new baby. For close on seven years I had enjoyed the undivided attention of my parents and relatives, and been made a fuss of in a large extended family. Now, all at once, things had changed and it was difficult for me to adjust to the new situation.

Initially, my reactions to Maureen's birth had been ones of excitement and pride. Like many an older child who does not yet understand the full implications of a new arrival in the family, I boasted to everyone about my baby sister. But as the weeks went by, it began to dawn on me that the new baby took up a large amount of Mum's time and that consequently she had less of it for me.

Gradually, I began to find solace by retreating into a world deep within myself. Whereas some children might have been openly jealous and become naughty, disobedient, or very demanding, I withdrew into my own private world where no-one could intrude. It was a secret world in which I could escape from reality and where I had complete control. I spent a great deal of time by myself, living out fantasies and playing games which involved spying on people or hiding items in secret places.

As well as my own "secret" world, there was another world that seemed to open up to me at this time, too. The countryside surrounding my home was not in any way "secret", but it provided me with many places to explore, and it was inhabited by countless numbers of animals, birds and insects that fascinated me.

Both "worlds" served the same purpose — they enabled me to cope with losing my position as the only child in the family.

Two years after Maureen was born, a traumatic event occurred which shook the whole family and could have easily ended in tragedy. It all began one afternoon as I arrived home from primary school. I had dawdled through the allotments with my friends as usual and, on opening the front door, found baby Maureen lying on the settee with some of her clothing removed. She was screaming loudly and Mum was bending over her in a highly agitated state.

As soon as I walked in through the front door Mum turned towards me.

"Go and fetch your Dad," she said abruptly. "Tell him to come home immediately — there's been an accident."

So off I went. Reluctantly I retraced my steps towards the centre of the village until I reached the Co-operative Shoe Department. Then going round the back and up the stairs to where Dad did his cobbling, I passed on Mum's message.

I have to admit I did not hurry. I was unaware of any sense of urgency. In fact, I remember that although Dad threw off his apron and rushed home as requested, I followed on behind, arriving several minutes after him. When I did get home however, it was obvious that the situation was serious.

Maureen had been toddling round the kitchen, following Mum as she did her chores, when she had caught the flex of the electric kettle with her arm and pulled it off the cooker. It had been full of boiling water and had poured its contents down my sister's side including her arm and leg. As Mum had taken off her clothes, a considerable amount of skin had come off with them.

The doctor was called and came immediately. He advised admittance to hospital as, if Maureen's life was to be saved, she would need twenty-four hour, round-the-clock nursing. Mum wouldn't hear of it. Determined to avoid a hospital admission, she decided that my sister would be nursed at home and that she and Dad would do all that was necessary.

The family was called in to help and the house was swiftly re-organised. The dining table and settee were pushed against one of the walls and Maureen's cot was brought downstairs and placed in the centre of our living room. Boxes of dressings were delivered by the district nurse, who said she would call in every day, and these were placed along the sideboard. For the next six weeks Mum and Dad played a major part in caring for my sister. They took it in turns to sit up with her, changed her dressings every four hours day and night, and saw to her every need. In time, she fully recovered and was left with only faint scars on her arm.

Although this was admirable and showed my parents' dedication and care, I now wonder whether this episode may have increased my sense of isolation. Whilst the nursing was taking place, and for several weeks afterwards during my sister's convalescence, the attention of my parents — and that of the larger family — was focused on Maureen.

Through my immature eyes, it it would appear that she was getting all the attention, all the care, all the love, all the physical contact — and I would feel even more deprived of these things.

However, I must not give the impression that I was antagonistic towards Maureen, or that I did not care about her. It was just that when she came into the world I was no longer the centre of attention in the family and, as there was a great age difference between us and we were at different stages of development, we could not play together or have shared interests as children. My role was often defined as her "big brother" with the duty of looking after my little sister, rather than having her as a playmate.

One way in which I had to care for my sister was to take her along to parties! As a small child, Maureen was shy in certain situations and this showed itself in unexpected ways. Often, when she was four or five years old, she would be invited to the birthday parties of playmates from Laneside, and later chums from school. Although initially she always seemed happy about the invitations, when the time came to go to the party she usually dissolved into floods of tears and refused to leave the house. No amount of coaxing would convince her that she would have a wonderful time, so eventually she was taken there in tears and "handed in at the door"!

On several occasions, this final duty was delegated to me and I remember clearly walking to parties alongside her, as she sobbed and protested that she didn't want to go. The strange thing was that on returning home two hours later, she always declared that she had had a great time, and would enjoy going to the next one!

By this time, I had moved up into the Junior Department at Littleborough Central Board School. In those days all education — from five to fifteen years — took place in the same building. After spending my first three years in the Department labelled "Infants" under the care of Miss Cockcroft, the headmistress, I had now made the transition into the "Big School", ruled over by a headmaster, Mr Bolam. He was known to us all as "Jazz Jay" as his signature was *Jas. J. Bolam*. Here I came into contact with older boys and girls, and learned that there were a number of teachers who were not averse to using the strap.

Although I do not recall having much difficulty at first with the move, when I was about eight or nine — a significant age in terms of my family circumstances — things began to go wrong. For a time in the second junior class we had a temporary teacher by the name of Mrs Newall who seemed to have little idea of how to interest children. She used to encourage us — Mr Squeers fashion — by threatening us that if we misbehaved we would "get the stick'!

The implement to which she referred was, in fact, the blackboard pointer, a polished wooden implement that resembled a miniature billiard cue. Depending on the seriousness of our misdemeanours, Mrs Newall would select either the "thin end" or the "thick end" of this instrument and deliver a blow across our palms with it. Somehow or other, I managed to receive one of these corrective treatments at regular intervals, but instead of encouraging me to "do better" as intended, it made me resentful and subversive.

Mrs Newall's departure came as a welcome relief for us all, but her successor, Mrs England — wife of the eccentric village chemist — was not a great improvement. It was she who gave the first indication to my parents that I was not always co-operative and obedient at school by writing the words "rather heedless" at the foot of my annual report. Although I did not know the meaning of the phrase, I remember that my parents were somewhat alarmed by it. Eventually, however, finding it difficult to believe that their quiet conformist son was capable of behaving in any other way, they were dismissive of both the comment and its author.

As I progressed through the junior classes, I became increasingly aware that something of importance was looming on the horizon — namely, the "eleven plus" examination. Whereas in the past everyone had seemed happy that I should develop at my own pace, suddenly it became important that I should do well.

Now, if I happened to tell Mum and Dad that I couldn't understand the teacher's explanations, they told me to ask — and ask again — until all became clear. If I was foolish enough to mention that I had got low marks in a test, they insisted I should try harder as my future would be affected by the result of the approaching examination. In the event, my future was affected by the examination but not primarily by the result. The tension and competition that surrounded it damaged my self-esteem and lowered my sense of self-worth.

However, in contrast to my antipathy towards school, my interest in the countryside grew stronger and stronger, and I became particularly fascinated by ants. Ants' nests, which could be found in various places near my home, were usually discovered by lifting a stone. I have since seen large, dome-shaped anthills at the side of Scottish lanes made from thousands of tiny twigs, but the red ants of my childhood seemed to prefer simpler abodes. Along the sandy banks of the stream near Greenhill Methodist Chapel there were several ants' nests. Often, on the way back from Sunday school, I would lift a large slab of millstone grit and watch the sudden burst of activity take place beneath it as I did so. Thousands of tiny red bodies would rapidly change up into fourth gear and scurry about a dozen different tasks. Some would pick up a pupa and struggle with it down the nearest hole. Others would gather in a group and touch antennae. Yet others would grab the nearest fragment of root or stalk and rush off with it in a panic. All seemed to have a role in life — even if the result did appear to be organised chaos!

I was captivated by these creatures. I think the idea of a society in which every member had a definite role, and where there was complete co-operation, appealed to me. Perhaps watching these insects go about their routine tasks compensated for the fact that I felt I had lost my unique position in my own family. One of my major ambitions at the time was to own a colony and keep it in my bedroom. This is not quite as outrageous as it sounds, for there was a description of how to make and maintain an "Ant Palace" in one of the old Christmas Annuals which had been handed down to me by my grandparents.

The method advocated involved fixing together two large panes of glass about half an inch apart, sealing the edges with wax, and filling the space in between with dry sand. Then, having introduced a community of ants into the "palace" — which had to contain a queen — one merely provided a mixture of honey and water at a designated feeding place, and watched them build passages, living areas, a nursery, a laying chamber for the queen and so on.

However, in spite of several attempts, I never succeeded in making a viable "Ant Palace". This was because, not having a spade, I could never manage to capture a queen, who stays well below ground level in the centre of the nest. But my fascination with the tiny creatures continued for many years and continues to this day.

My other great interest was birds. At the time, I used to listen to Children's Hour, which was broadcast every day at 5p.m. on the radio. One of my favourite programmes was called "Wandering with Nomad", which was a series in which two young girls, Muriel and Doris, were taken on walks through the countryside by a wise countryman, "Nomad". During these "walks" they observed and learned about all kinds of wild creatures.

One day they would come upon a number of fox cubs play-fighting close to their den, and Nomad would explain how they were preparing for a life of hunting and catching their prey. On another occasion they would find a hedgehog rolling in a pile of Autumn leaves, and Nomad would tell Muriel and Doris that it was about to hibernate in a hole between the roots of a tree until spring. Or perhaps they would chance upon three or four baby hares crouching in a set as they walked across a field. Nomad would suggest hiding behind a nearby hedge and they would see the mother return to feed them, watching as she leapt into the air periodically to break the scent trail in case she was being followed by a stoat or another predator.

However, I soon realised as I wandered through the fields and woods around Calderbrook Road that Nomad had been extremely fortunate to see so many wild creatures during his country walks. I saw very few! But I did begin to notice many different kinds of birds, and their varied habits and habitats. I decided to keep a record of the ones I had seen, and make a note of where I had seen them.

I bought a book: "Birds of Britain", and spent ages wandering along country lanes looking in hedgerows for nests in the hope of finding a clutch of eggs or some developing chicks. Unfortunately, most of the nests I came across had already been torn apart by other children who had stolen the eggs — and this upset me and made me want to take revenge on the perpetrators.

Eventually, offended by these acts of vandalism, I took to the hills surrounding the village, which were inhabited by skylarks and meadow pipits. But although this environment was less attractive to the egg-stealers, the nests were much more difficult to find. Consequently, I discovered that virtually the only way of locating a skylark's nest was to almost step on a sitting bird. If a skylark flew up from my feet, I knew I was in with a chance! Unlikely though it may seem, this did happen on a number of occasions, but having found a nest in this way, there was a further problem to overcome. Because it was very difficult to mark a nest's position in the huge expanse of moorland, often I could not find it again when I returned at a later date.

My interest in the countryside grew even more when, during one school holiday just after my ninth birthday, Auntie Ethel and Uncle Charlie asked me if I would like to accompany them on a holiday.

"Where are we going?" I asked.

"Why, to Leintwardine, of course, to see George and Maggie."

"What's it like?"

"Oh, it's wonderful. You'll see lots of rabbits — and there are no electric lights!"

As a small child I had often heard my relatives talk about Leintwardine. I knew that it was a village in Shropshire that had some connection with our family, and that Auntie Nellie visited it every year. On several occasions I had heard her say that she would like to live there. I also knew that every December my parents sent a Christmas card to a family in Leintwardine, addressed to:

Mr and Mrs Howells,
   36, Watling Street,
      Leintwardine,
         Craven Arms,
           Bucknell,
              Salop.

but I had no idea what the relationship was between ourselves and the recipients of the Christmas greetings.

Much later in life, I pieced together some of the history. Grandad and Grandma Broome had both been born in Shropshire in the 1870s and, having met and fallen in love, had both left Leintwardine to seek employment. Grandma got a job as a domestic servant in a large house in Great Warford, Cheshire, and Grandad was employed by one of the newly-developing railway companies. The records show they were married in Alderley Edge, Cheshire, in 1900, and that Grandad's profession at the time was a "pointsman".

Soon after they married, Grandma became pregnant, so the couple lodged with her elder sister who was living on a farm in Littleborough. She, too, had been in domestic service in the north of England but had had the good fortune to marry a farmer and move into his farmhouse as his wife. My grandparents' first child — Uncle Charlie — was born whilst they were lodging there, but by the time my father came along in 1904 they had rented a house of their own and settled in Littleborough. Grandad left the railway company and became a carter for a local firm that made glazed earthenware pipes.

However, Grandma Broome had some married sisters that had remained in Shropshire, and it was with some of their children that contact had been maintained and letters and cards were exchanged.

None of this was known to me as I set off with Ethel and Charlie one day on the long journey to Leintwardine. Carrying our suitcases, we boarded the train from Littleborough to Manchester, where we had to change for Shrewsbury. Following this, we took a local train to Craven Arms, and from there we had to rely on a country bus which ran, I seem to remember, at two-hourly intervals.

When we arrived at Leintwardine however, I found everything about it enchanting. To begin with, it was truly rural, being made up of only two narrow streets formed in the shape of a letter "Y". Neither had continuous footpaths along their length nor any streetlights to illuminate them after dark.

The village was set in open, rolling countryside and at its lower end, where the two roads joined, was a stone, triple-arched bridge over the river Teme. The village boasted two country inns — "The Lion" and "The Swan" — one on each arm of the "Y", and there was a lovely stone church with a square tower which nestled between them in the heart of the village.

As we walked down Watling Street, having alighted from the bus, I felt as if I had been transported to a magical land. Everyone we passed acknowledged our presence with an "'Ow be ye?" and when we eventually reached our destination, the cottage seemed so small and so low that one almost felt one could stand on tiptoe and knock on the upstairs windows!

The Howell family were all there to greet us. A short plump woman with a ruddy complexion and flyaway greying hair was introduced as "Auntie Mag", and her husband, wearing a striped blue collarless shirt and trousers held up by bracers, was "Uncle George". Their daughters, both much older than me, were introduced as Vera and Nellie. "But we call her 'Little Nellie'," added Mag, "so she don't get mixed up with your auntie." (Nellie Broome.)

Their cottage was built side-on to the street and right next to it was their long garden, filled with rows of vegetables and all kinds of soft fruit. Just beyond the washhouse was an old apple tree.

I knew immediately that I was going to enjoy my stay in Leintwardine.

CHAPTER
FIVE

Pleasure and Pain

George and Mag's living room was furnished with an assortment of comfortable but well-worn furniture. There were two armchairs, a deal table, a Welsh dresser full of plates, three or four dining chairs and a set of cupboards built into an alcove beside the window. The fire was contained in a black cast-iron grate. Above it was a mantleshelf packed with ornaments, and beneath it a rectangular enamelled sheet surrounded by a black fender. A multicoloured peg rug completed the fireside scene.

Around the walls were a number of very large pictures in ornate frames depicting country scenes, and the ceiling was so low that a man of average height could easily reach up and touch it. From the back left hand corner of the room a staircase led up to the second floor, and located beneath it, visible through an archway to the left, was the kitchen.

It had been decided in advance that I could not sleep at George and Mag's cottage, as they had only one room upstairs divided into two sections by a partition. So almost immediately I was taken to Ted and Edie's house, a short distance along a lane on the opposite side of Watling Street. Ted and Edie were brother and sister (and even more distant relatives of ours) but they made me feel at home, giving me a small single room overlooking their garden. I then returned to George and Mag's house for the rest of the day.

It was a day full of surprises. Uncle George showed me the toilet — of the tub variety — at the far end of the garden, and explained the rule about evening visits ("Switch the torch on to get there and back, but switch it off whilst sitting on"). And when evening came I watched as a large paraffin lamp was placed in the centre of the table and lit. When the glass bowl was replaced and the flame had steadied, the room was filled with a strong clear light. Then a pack of playing cards was produced and the rest of the evening was spent in playing various games.

I soon grew accustomed to Leintwardine and its different lifestyle. I enjoyed the long walks along country lanes with Ethel and Charlie, but it was George and Ted who educated me in country ways.

At the time, I had never seen a wild rabbit and was thrilled to see dozens of them at dusk feeding in the fields near the hedgerows. However, my interest was not confined to observation, for I had seen one or two local men returning home with a pair of rabbits over their shoulders, and I too was keen to catch one for the pot. George knew the location of every warren within a mile of his home and in the evening, when they were out of their burrows feeding, he would show me how to move towards them so that they did not take fright. He taught me that a rabbit's first defence when threatened is to "freeze" on the spot, and one could often get within a yard or two before the creature bolted. I practised this a few times and proved it to be true.

Then he showed me his catapult. Of course I had seen catapults before — great forked twigs and lengths of white knicker-elastic owned by boys at home — but Uncle George's catapult was in a different league. It was a deadly weapon. Made out of cherry wood and fitting comfortably into the palm of his hand, it had solid square-section elastic and a leather stone-holder. Cupping the fork between his index finger and thumb, he could hit a rabbit at five yards. Then, running forward to where it was stunned, he would finish it off with a blow of his walking stick.

As I write this now, his behaviour sounds cruel, but one has to remember that the rabbit was classed as a serious pest by country people as it ate and destroyed many of their crops. It also made a free, tasty meal for people who were not high earners. In fact, a few years later, when I visited Leintwardine at harvest time, I joined the entire male population of the village in a rabbit hunt. A field of wheat was being mown and as the mowing machine gradually worked its way from the perimeter to the centre of the field, the rabbits hiding in the grain were trapped in the middle. A crowd of men round the field's edge, armed with walking sticks, moved inward as the machine completed each circuit, and when the rabbits made a dash from their cover, many were killed and taken home.

Eventually, Ted made a catapult for me and in order to practise I put a tin can on the wall of his garden and tried to knock it off. The following day he came upon a dead sparrow on the ground and propped it on a branch with a twig to make a more realistic target for me to aim at!

Almost every day at Leintwardine I discovered something new. One day, when we all decided to go for a stroll along a country lane, I was surprised to see both George and Mag carrying a walking stick. When I asked the reason for this, George just winked and said, "Wait and see."

After half a mile or so, they paused and began to reach up and use them to strike the branches of certain trees in the hedge. Little clusters of brown nuts began to fall on to the lane and, on picking them up, I found they were similar to the hazel nuts we had at Grandma Broome's Christmas parties.

"They're cobnuts," explained George. "Do you good. All you need is a pair of nutcrackers!"

I learned on a future visit that the curved handles of walking sticks were also very useful for pulling down the high arching stems of brambles when one went on a blackberrying expedition.

I had been sleeping at Ted and Edie's for a couple of days before I happened to glance up at the ceiling above their front door. There, high up on the wall, resting on two wooden pegs, was a double-barrelled shotgun. Seeing me looking at it, Ted took it down, showed me how it worked, and explained where the cartridges were placed. I never saw him use it, but it was certainly in good working order and I am sure that many of the pheasants wandering about the fields were in great danger at certain times of year.

Another day, on rising early, I happened to go into Ted's room to ask him a question. Imagine my total shock to find a full-size human leg — from foot to thigh — standing next to his bed! Seeing the amazed (and no doubt horror-stricken) look on my face, he explained that he had had his real leg shot off in the First World War and as he could not wear a false one in bed, he took it off every night. Although I had noticed that Ted used a walking stick, and swung one leg rather awkwardly, it had never occurred to me that he did not have two legs of his own.

One day, as I was walking along a lane with Uncle George, my bare legs brushed against a clump of nettles causing me considerable discomfort. George hunted around until he found some dock leaves, which he rubbed on my nettle rash making my legs quite green.

"That'll fix it," he said, "In a minute or two the stinging will stop." His prediction was true, but whether it was due to the dock leaves or what I witnessed next, I'll never know. "The thing about nettles," continued Uncle George, "is that you've got to show 'em who's boss. If you get hold of 'em like this — tight — they won't hurt you." And with that he leant over the patch of nettles and with a strong, upward grasping movement, took a great handful of stems and pulled them free of the clump.

"Come on, then, have a go," he invited me, but I have to confess that my apprehension was stronger than my courage, and I did not rise to the challenge. Nevertheless, I was so taken up with the episode that I did not notice the stinging on my legs for the rest of the walk.

One evening, George told us all — Uncle Charlie, Auntie Ethel and me — that the following morning we would be going to gather mushrooms as there were plenty about at the moment. It involved rising very early and setting out before breakfast, as he assured us that if we left it until later they would all be gone. At the time, I got the impression that they somehow dissolved in the first rays of the morning sun, but I have since wondered whether he meant they would all have been taken by other early risers like ourselves.

However, early the following morning, armed with wicker baskets, we set off towards a wooded area a short distance from the village. Under the trees amongst the leaf-mould were lots of fungi, and we had to learn quickly which were edible and which were poisonous. Uncle George could tell at a glance which were genuine mushrooms — "Look for the black fins underneath" — and which were toadstools, but the rest of us were unsure at times and had to ask his advice. I'm afraid I was not a great deal of help to the adults as I became fascinated by "puff-balls", spherical fungi that discharged clouds of brown spores when I touched them.

When we had collected a good supply of mushrooms, we all returned home for a full English breakfast — and I am sure you do not need to guess which part of the meal we thought was the most tasty.

★ ★ ★

I did not see a great deal of Vera or "Little Nellie" during my stay in Leintwardine. Vera had left the village school at fifteen, and was employed as a nanny by the village doctor and his wife, so she was rarely at home. Initially she had two children to care for, but when a third, disabled child was born, her role grew in importance. Vera worked long hours, but became deeply committed to the doctor's family. In return, they treated her as "one of the family", took her on holiday with them and regarded her with affection and respect.

"Little Nellie" was a bright girl and left the village to train as a nurse, staying in a nurses' hostel in the Midlands. She returned to Leintwardine frequently for holidays and to see her family, but did not settle in the village again. She showed an aptitude for the career she had chosen and eventually became a sister and ultimately the matron of a children's hospital in Birmingham.

Tragically, Nellie died in her mid-fifties, having had a bad dose of influenza which eventually gave rise to septicaemia. Vera remained single and lived in the same cottage in Leintwardine until she was an old woman, when she had to move into a Rest Home in a neighbouring town.

However, there were many village characters that I did see on a regular basis. Grandpa Barnett was an old man who could always be found on the same bench in the same place in the village every day. He had a nut-brown complexion and an enormous bushy beard stained yellow by smoking his long-stemmed pipe. One day as I passed him with Uncle George, we paused and George introduced me.

"Arnold Broome's lad," he said briefly, nodding towards me. "Come down with Ethel and Charlie. Staying at Ted's."

The old man nodded and smiled at me, and then we went on our way. It was many years later that I learnt there was a story involving the Broomes and the Barnetts.

Apparently, as a young woman, Auntie Nellie had often visited Leintwardine. She was attracted by the countryside and the country way of life. In addition, she got on well with Vera and Little Nellie, and was actually thinking of moving back to the place of her parents' birth.

During her visits, she was spotted by a young man called Donald Barnett, the old man's son, who took a fancy to her and began to make amorous advances towards her. I am not sure how the relationship developed — but his feelings must have been reciprocated to some extent as I have an old photograph in my possession showing the two of them sitting side by side on a bench, with Donald's arm around Nellie.

Many years later, Dad told me that Donald had made the long journey to Littleborough to ask Grandad Broome for Nellie's hand in marriage. Whether or not permission was given I am not sure, but the relationship did not develop any further and there were no wedding bells. In later years, it was generally thought by the family that Nellie had been put off men

by seeing the way her father had treated her mother —
coming home drunk whilst she struggled to bring up a
large family. If that was the case, poor Donald didn't
have a chance. It is certainly true that throughout all
my childhood years Nellie never had an association
with a man, but preferred the company of women of
her own age with whom she worked.

My idyllic stay in Leintwardine passed all too quickly
and inevitably the time came for my return to
Littleborough. Reluctantly I packed my suitcase, said
goodbye to the country folk who had made me feel so
welcome, and accompanied Auntie Ethel and Uncle
Charlie on the return journey north. Soon I was home
again, surrounded by my family and caught up in the
everyday cycle of events. It was back to the reality of
the familiar routine of home life, and the customary
staleness of school.

Alongside my formal schooling, the pattern of which
varied from year to year, I began to realise I possessed
one natural talent which was always with me. I was very
good at drawing. Whereas other children's pictures of
horses, aeroplanes or people were often barely
recognisable, my efforts were fairly lifelike and admired
by all.

I first became aware of this ability when I was eight
or nine years old. Returning home from school one
afternoon, I went to play at the home of an older boy
who had moved into the house next to the post office
on Laneside. I was surprised to find him sitting on the
floor in front of the biggest piece of paper I had ever

seen. On it was the most wonderful sketch of a "dog-fight" between Spitfires and enemy aircraft. There were planes diving and swooping in all directions and shells bursting around them from the anti-aircraft guns below.

Watching his pencil moving over the paper and creating a scene which was full of movement and vitality really excited me — and I remember wanting to be able to do the same.

At first, I tended to copy the things he drew and became expert at producing fighter planes in all angles of attack, but gradually the subject matter widened and I experimented in other areas. I began to draw action scenes or dramatic events — a dozen cowboys attacking a tribe of Indians, or a platoon of soldiers advancing on the enemy. The style was cartoon-like and the picture told a story which was being worked out on the page.

Being able to draw brought me popularity with my peers. Sometimes at school, a group of children would gather round me and watch me produce one of my masterpieces, contributing their ideas as to where I should place the next Spitfire or which Indian should be the next to bite the dust. At other times, some of my classmates would ask me to make a sketch in their exercise book to illustrate the written work on the opposite page. At last I had found something I was good at, so I was always willing to oblige.

When it came to passing the eleven-plus however, being able to draw did not figure highly amongst the required attributes. More emphasis was placed on English, Mathematics and Intelligence!

In those days, children whose birthdays fell during the Summer holiday in August — which mine did — could have two bites of the cherry. With the teacher's approval, such children could be entered in the examination a "year early", as they would have had their eleventh birthday by the time they went to the grammar school. They could also be entered the following year when they were still eleven plus, but had not yet made up twelve.

As my birthday is on the 6th August, I was allowed to take the examination a year early. One or two other children did the same, including Gerald Pickering, my regular playmate on Laneside, who shared my date of birth. However, when the results came out several weeks later, I found that although I had failed the test, Gerald had passed for grammar school at his first attempt.

I cannot remember how I reacted to the news that I had not been successful. I imagine that I withdrew into my world of fantasy and blotted the whole thing out of my mind. Nevertheless, during the summer holiday period that year, whilst Gerald was being kitted out with a new school uniform and satchel in order to move on, I had to face returning to the Central School for another year.

To give my parents their due, after the test results were announced Mum and Dad tried to be positive and encouraging, but they were obviously disappointed. During the next twelve months, although Mum was not able to give me any practical help with my schoolwork, she did her best to instil confidence.

"If you *think* you can do something," she would say, whenever I expressed self-doubt, "you will find that you *can!* The trouble with you is that you have an '*inferiority complex*'." Despite having little idea of the meaning of the phrase, she had diagnosed my problem with some accuracy.

Looking back now, it is easy to see why I began to develop a negative view of myself. At home, I was still coming to terms with sharing the limelight with my sister, and at school it appeared I was not as intelligent or clever as one of my close friends. However, there was no opportunity for me to share these feelings, and had I been given the chance to do so, I could not have articulated them. So there was nothing for it but to return to the Central School for another year and wait for the eleven-plus to come round again.

The following year I passed the examination — but this time I was one of the oldest candidates taking the test. My success meant that instead of moving into the Senior Department at the Central Board School and leaving at the age of fifteen to work in the mill or take up an apprenticeship, I would transfer to grammar school and stay on to take "O" levels with the prospect of a professional career ahead.

There were two Lancashire County grammar schools from which I could choose, neither of which was very close to my home. They were Heywood Grammar School, some seven and a half miles away in Heywood, and The Queen Elizabeth Grammar School in Middleton, which was at least eight miles from Littleborough. Both involved a journey on two buses.

In the end my parents opted for the former, partly because it was slightly closer to my home and partly because many of my contemporaries had made that choice.

Heywood Grammar School was a tall, rectangular, three-storey, brick building overlooking the Memorial Gardens in the centre of Heywood. Whilst its educational provision may well have been superior to that provided by Littleborough Central School, its architecture and facilities were not in the same league. In a former life it had served as a Municipal Technical School, for those were the words embossed on a coat of arms in the brickwork near its roof.

The lower floor, which housed a number of classrooms and the woodwork room, was in fact a basement. Being below street level, these rooms were very gloomy and the electric lights were rarely switched off. Occasionally, whilst sitting in a French lesson or pondering over a problem in maths, one would glance up to see a group of pensioners or young mums with prams staring down at one from the pavement which ran alongside the school.

The main entrance, approached by climbing a flight of stone steps under a curved stone arch, led to the middle floor. Just inside the swing doors was the head's room, and on this floor were the assembly hall which doubled as a gym, the school office, and the cookery room where the girls did Domestic Science. The upper floor housed the Physics and Chemistry laboratories, the library and, directly opposite the top of the staircase, the art room. This was a very light and airy room as it had large windows along one entire wall. It was said that it was originally used for Technical Drawing.

There was no provision for dining. When lunchtime came, the entire school had to form an enormous crocodile and walk to a canteen about a quarter of a mile away, which was housed in a couple of prefabricated buildings on the other side of Heywood centre. A similar procedure applied on our Games afternoon. The school sports field was about a third of a mile in the opposite direction, so in this case we had to carry our kit through the streets before taking part in games. The playing field contained a hut in which to change but lacked any washing facilities, so after a midwinter game of football, we had to return to school covered in mud and do the best we could to get clean in the school cloakroom before catching the bus home.

The teachers at the Grammar School were thought to be a cut above the masters and mistresses in the Central School. To begin with, they all wore black gowns. The only exception to this was on Speech Day when they came dressed in their full regalia consisting of robes trimmed with coloured fur. The staff called all the boys by their surnames, (although the same rule did not apply to the girls) and the boys, in turn, called all the teachers by appropriate nicknames. So Mr Hope became "Soapy", Mr Thorne was called "Spike", Mr Halstead the woodwork teacher was known as "Chisel", and the Chemistry teacher, Mr G. A. Gregory, was known as "Gag". For some unknown reason, Mr Hawarth, the Geography specialist, had the nickname of "Collops" — and this caused me some embarrassment one day when I went to the staff room and asked for him by this name. I still don't know what it means!

Even before my first visit to the school, I had been petrified by tales circulating among my peer group regarding the "welcoming rituals" that we had to undergo as "new kids". There were "crop fights" arranged by older pupils in which two newcomers were coerced into slapping each other across the back of the head until one of them was reduced to tears — a kind of "conkers" game using the human cranium as a target. There was the pastime of pushing the heads of first year pupils down the toilet, preferably after it had been used, and holding them there whilst the chain was pulled. Add to these other diversions of the senior boys, such as throwing new kids' caps or plimsolls on the roof of the bike shed at playtimes and it is easy to see why the first weeks at Heywood Grammar School were something of a nightmare.

I lasted for three days. Before the first week was out, I had begun to feel ill every morning. The fourth day found me at home, resisting my parents' exhortations to "give as good as I got", and declaring that I was "sick". Indeed I was — sick with fear, and already sick of my new school.

I was absent for about a week, and although the initial outbreak of bullying had diminished by the time I returned, I had missed much of the introductory work which had been done by the teachers.

I was placed in the B stream of the three-class first year, and stayed in this middle grade for my entire school career. Although at first many of the new subjects contained a certain novel appeal, after a month or two I found the educational programme tedious and uninspiring. There was a continual emphasis on rote-learning and the focus was on the assimilation of facts rather than the development of skills. In addition, the constant preoccupation with making comparisons between pupils only served to reinforce the negative view that I had of myself and confirm that I was a poor learner. Forty years passed before I realised that my mental ability lay in *remembering processes* rather than *retaining facts*, and that creativity was one of my greatest assets.

Life as a grammar school pupil brought many changes. For example my "school day" became considerably longer. Instead of the ten-minute walk to the Central School in the centre of the village, I had to make the eight-mile journey to Heywood. Whilst this trip normally took about forty-five minutes using the special School Bus Service, if I was delayed for any reason — either morning or evening — it could take up to an hour and a half. So I would often leave home by eight o'clock in the morning and seldom return home before five in the afternoon.

Another new feature was homework, which was supplied complete with a homework diary for my parents to sign each week. Although I began with good intentions, it was not long before I was doing my homework on the bus as I travelled to school in the morning, or copying it from some willing friend during the playtime immediately preceding the lesson. Looking back now, I realise that I never really engaged in the educative process that the grammar school provided. My unhappy start at the school, my poor self-image and my fear of failure caused me to withdraw from challenges and shy away from all competition.

In common with many other children from working class backgrounds who gained places in higher education, I also found that my programme of work at grammar school began to separate me from my "roots". Although Mum and Dad were literate and full of common sense, their education had been only basic. Our house contained hardly any books and there were never any discussions on philosophical or cultural matters. Aspects of mathematics such as algebra or geometry, and the grammatical analysis of written English were beyond their comprehension. French, Latin, Physics and Chemistry were absolutely "closed books".

So as I began to make progress in these areas, my parents became simultaneously proud and confused — proud of my achievements (limited though they were) but confused by the content of the lessons. They found it impossible to give help with my homework, so their main input was to encourage me to "try hard" and "do well". They continually reminded me that *they* had never had such a wonderful opportunity, and I should make the most of it.

I discovered that my educational knowledge provided me with a certain degree of power. As my parents knew little about the subjects being taught, they soon lost touch with my educational progress. And because the grammar school was over seven miles from home (and telephones were not in general use), they had few opportunities to consult with the teachers. Consequently, I found myself able to withhold information that it was not in my interest to divulge — and to manipulate or falsify accounts of events to suit my own ends.

The secret inner world into which I had retreated to find solace as a younger child now became a place where I would conjure up my own view of reality and promote it as the truth. My subversive self remained alive and well, co-existing alongside the conformist and conventional persona which I presented to the world. But even though duality was becoming my regular way of coping with life, I was still very unhappy and had a low opinion of myself.

Looking back now, I find it difficult to remember what I did in my leisure time. We were not the sort of family who always had a jigsaw on the go, or played cards or dominoes together in the evening. Occasionally at weekends we would get out the "Snakes and Ladders" or the "Ludo" board, but in retrospect I seem to have spent a great deal of my time in withdrawing from reality and daydreaming. I was helped in this by regular visits to the cinema — often alone. As a small child I had been to the Saturday matinees to watch cowboy and Indian films with my friends, but now I went to evening performances, although always to the "first house" which began at about 6.15p.m.

There were two cinemas in Littleborough. The "Victoria" was in Sale Street, quite close to the Central

School, and the "Queens" was on Church Street near the village centre and the bus terminus. Both had two performances each evening, and a change of programme on Mondays and Thursdays, so it was possible to see four different films in one week if one wished.

Fairly regularly, I would escape into the realms of fantasy as I watched George Formby, Tarzan of the Apes, Frank Randle, or Abbott and Costello getting into one scrape after another, but eventually outwitting the enemy and coming out on top! As I walked up Hare Hill Road on my way home, I would imagine myself into a similar position to that of the film hero I had just seen, and embark upon a flight of fancy in which I overcame all opposition and ended up victorious.

I am not sure whether it was the influence of my parents or the persuasion of Brian Carter, a school friend from further along Calderbrook Road, but at about this time I decided to join the scout troupe associated with Littleborough Parish Church. After a trial period of a week or two, my parents bought me a uniform and I went through the initiation ceremony of swearing my loyalty to God and the King, and promising to help someone everyday.

Our weekly meetings were held in a scout hut on Ealees Road, which had a field alongside it where we could camp and do various outdoor activities during the summer months. In the Scouts, I learned the various skills and techniques for survival, such as how to pitch a tent, make a fire by rubbing two sticks together, set up a camp kitchen and dig a hygienic loo.

I also learned how to tie a whole range of knots, many of which I remember to this day but have rarely used.

However, when it came to the team games that were organised for our enjoyment, I found many of them too rough as most of them seemed to be a cross between wrestling and rugby league. My personal nightmare was one called "British Bulldog". This involved dividing the troupe into two teams, one team trying to run from one end of the Scout hut to the other, whilst the second team did everything in its power to stop them. Bruises and bloody noses were not regular features of this game, but occurred often enough to put me off it for life.

Gradually my interest waned and I began to attend meetings less frequently. Eventually, I heard from a friend that any scout missing three consecutive meetings would have to explain his absence. Not having attended for several weeks I was summoned to appear in uniform before a special "Court of Honour" and, as I could not provide a satisfactory explanation for my non-attendance, was dismissed from the troupe.

I have often joked about the matter since, marvelling at how "conforming" I was in turning up to be dismissed! I still find it amusing that my punishment for non-attendance was expulsion from the troupe. It seems a bit like refusing to feed an anorexic!

When I was twelve, I developed an interest in photography. It all began one Saturday afternoon when I was visiting Grandma Broome's house. I had been there only a short time when Auntie Nellie opened a drawer, took out a small, oblong, canvas case and put it on the table in front of me.

"Would you like this?" she asked. "I don't use it any more."

Inside the case was a soft leather pouch and inside that was a neat, compact folding camera. On its side was printed "Vest Pocket Kodak" and on the front, around the lens, were levers which allowed one to alter the shutter speed, and change the size of the aperture. A pull on the front opened the bellows and it was ready to take a picture. At that time, many families owned a Box Brownie that was used on high days and holidays to take snaps, but this was a precision instrument which was small enough to fit in one of my pockets. I thanked Auntie Nellie profusely and accepted the gift immediately!

Photography was an ideal hobby for me at this stage in my life as it was an individual pastime (as opposed to a team activity), and it also allowed me to express myself creatively through my pictures.

Although I enjoyed composing and taking photographs, it was not long before I wanted to develop and print my own films, so I read up on the matter and discovered that in order to do this I needed a dark-room, lit only by a red light. The magazines suggested that this could be achieved by blacking out a bathroom, as water was readily available there, and suitable work-surfaces could be made from plywood and fitted over the wash-basin or the bath.

Unfortunately we did not have a bathroom, and as no other room in the house could be blacked out properly, it seemed as if I would be thwarted until I hit upon the idea of using the coal cellar.

The coal cellar was divided into two compartments. At the far end was a long, narrow chute with a manhole at ceiling level through which coal was tipped by the coal man, but in addition, at the bottom of the cellar steps, there was a rectangular area with a large, flat stone slab projecting from one of the walls. It looked as though it had been designed as a cold store on which to place food.

A bonus was that there was a lamp holder fitted to the wall above this slab so the area could be illuminated. The disadvantages were that the "room" was barely five feet high, and was very cold and damp.

Nevertheless, once I had got my parents' permission to use it, I set about transforming it into a dark-room. Into the lamp holder I plugged an extension so that it would take two bulbs — one red, one clear. I cleaned the slab and bought a developing tank, printing frame, and the flat dishes I required. In a matter of weeks I was in business!

Over the next few years I spent many happy hours taking pictures of people and places, and developing and printing them in my "dark-room". Although I had to carry warm water down the cellar steps before each session, and continually improvise when carrying out the various processes, I achieved reasonable results. After a while, I began to save up to buy an enlarger, but in fact I never got round to doing so. Perhaps it was the fact that as I grew older and taller it became more and more difficult to work in an area just five feet high, or perhaps other interests took over, but gradually I stopped doing my own processing, although I continued to take photographs.

At this time, only expensive cameras were fitted with flash provision, and even my Vest Pocket Kodak was not in that league. However, once again my creativity came to my aid and I worked out a way in which, with the aid of photo-flash bulbs, a battery and some wires, it *was* possible to take indoor pictures. And so I became the family's official amateur photographer and recorded several family celebrations — weddings, silver weddings and special birthdays — much to the delight of all concerned.

CHAPTER
SIX

Fear and Frustration

Two significant changes occurred in my home circumstances as I entered my teenage years: Mum returned to work and Grandma Ackroyd came to live with us.

Mum's new job was working alongside Dad. By this time Dad had settled into his role as manager of the Co-op Shoe Department and the move had proved to be a great success, both for the business and for Dad's own personal development. Within a year or two of his promotion the shop's profits had risen significantly and he had become a well-known figure, liked and respected by the many villagers who visited the shop.

Some time later, when old Sarah — the shop assistant who had worked for Dad's predecessor — retired, Dad had to find someone new to fill the vacancy. He did not have far to look, for Mum was ready and willing to step into the breach. And so began the many years of their successful co-operation at the Co-op.

Together the two of them gradually built up the business in the footwear department until frequently it made four or five times the "dividend" made by other shops in the Society. And their co-operation paid some personal dividends, too. Because Dad was Mum's boss, he was able to allow some flexibility in her working hours. Often, on a quiet day, he would let her slip out a little early to do some shopping or make the tea or, if my sister or myself were ill, he would allow her to arrive at work a bit later in the morning.

Conversely, when stocktaking time came, Mum would stay behind after hours to help him check and count the stock. In their working relationship Mum and Dad made a great partnership.

Mum's full-time employment created many opportunities for me to stay away from school. Since my transfer to grammar school I had become increasingly unhappy with school life, and I would often suffer from stomach pains in the morning at the prospect of a particular lesson. I remember many occasions when I complained of stomach-ache and refused to leave the house whilst Mum tried to persuade me that the day's programme would not be half as bad as I anticipated. Eventually however, she would have to leave for work. And as she departed — and the threat of school departed — my pain would gradually depart, too.

Looking back now, it is difficult for me to determine whether my physical symptoms were wholly psychosomatic. They certainly felt very real at the time. But the essential point is that I gradually learned that if I persisted in declaring that I was ill, I was able to avoid having to go to the much-hated school.

During my early years at grammar school, I was invariably absent with Mum's permission, but as I grew older I found more creative ways of playing truant. A friend and I devised a plan in which we would leave for school as usual but, after depositing our satchels in a left-luggage office in Rochdale, we would travel to Manchester and spend the day touring the large department stores, having lunch in Littlewoods' self-service restaurant.

Then, during the late afternoon we would return to Littleborough — retrieving our cases on the way — and arrive home with the other children, who never guessed that we had not been to school as they had. My parents never found out about these absences so once again my devious behaviour had a successful outcome.

The subversive side of my personality also came into play during my quest to get a pet. For many years I had wanted a kitten, but requests to my parents had always been met with a firm refusal. I couldn't understand it — it wasn't as though saying "yes" would have cost them any money. The cats at Grandad Broome's hen-pen were always having kittens, and it seemed perfectly reasonable to me that I should be allowed to keep one of these, if only to save it from the bucket.

Mum and Dad's argument had three main points:

- our house was too small for extra occupants
- they would end up looking after the animal, and
- I had a pet already.

It was true. I did have a pet. When I was about ten, in response to my continual pestering for an animal, I had been bought a budgerigar in a cage. After the initial

99

thrill of receiving it, I soon realised that a bird came second only to a goldfish in being an uninteresting pet — it could not be played with, taken for walks or cuddled. And to make matters worse, "Billy" turned out to be a most aggressive budgie who would peck your finger if you put it anywhere near the cage. So having relented once, my parents now seemed to have a cast-iron reason for refusing to allow another pet in the house — a bird and a kitten were incompatible.

One day, in the midst of my frustration and disappointment, a daring plan came into my head. At first, it alarmed me, because it came from my "subversive self", but if only I had the courage to carry it out, I reasoned, I could have a kitten in next to no time. The idea was simple. At least twice a week Billy was allowed out of his cage and given the freedom of the living room. Suppose that one day, whilst he was flying around, I "thoughtlessly" opened the front door and he flew out through it? I couldn't be blamed for an accident, could I? And then Billy would be gone for good!

For a while the "conformist" side of my personality would not entertain the idea. Although the plan was attractive and would undoubtedly work, I did not feel I had the courage to go through with it. And I was certain that I did not have the ability to act in a grief-stricken manner as I told my parents of Billy's "escape". But the subversive thoughts kept returning. If I really wanted a kitten, they insisted, I needed to put the plan into action. Otherwise, as budgies live to be twelve years old, I could say goodbye to a kitten forever.

Gradually, I built up my courage. As I lay in bed at night I would go over and over the plan, rehearsing every detail. I decided it would be best to let Billy "escape" one Saturday afternoon before Mum got home from work. That would give me time to calm myself afterwards, and prepare myself for my acting role.

In the event, everything went like a dream. On the chosen day, I let Billy out of his cage and watched him do a couple of circuits of the living room before landing on top of the wall-mirror, his usual perching place. Then, opening both the vestibule door and the front door, I encouraged him to fly round and round until he "found" the exit. As he disappeared over the rooftops of the houses opposite I experienced a wave of satisfaction which was immediately replaced by feelings of fear and trepidation as I waited for Mum to return home from work.

However, my acting performance must have been fairly convincing because, as far as I know, my parents never suspected the truth. Several weeks later, I was given permission to own a kitten, but it was never to become a family pet. One of the conditions that my parents set was that it should be kept at the hen-pen!

Grandma Ackroyd came to live with us during my second year at grammar school. Grandad Ackroyd had died several years earlier in November 1945 when I was eight years old, but I remember little of the event. I know that I did not attend his funeral, and I cannot recall any conversations about it or any expressions of grief in the family. Many years later, I learned that he had died of cancer of the rectum, and I suspect that it was a very painful death. My parents no doubt wanted to shield me from the horror they experienced when nursing him, and later when visiting him in hospital during the last few weeks of his life. The easiest way for them to do this was to remain silent in my presence and not talk about it at all.

However, about four years after Grandad's death, Grandma suffered a "seizure" (Mum's word) which, on top of her diabetes, meant that she needed help and support. So at Mum and Dad's invitation, she gave up her rented house and moved in with us. She was allocated to the back bedroom of our home in Calderbrook Road, and although this did not affect me — I slept in the attic — it meant that Maureen had to share my parents' room.

In fact, Grandma's presence in the house seemed to make little impact on me. I have a clear memory of her mouth turning down at one corner as a result of her stroke, and Mum massaging it with olive oil in an attempt to "get the use back into it", but I cannot recall many conversations, games played, or times enjoyed with Grandma Ackroyd. Perhaps she was too ill to be involved with an active thirteen-year-old.

Around my fourteenth birthday, Grandma's health took a turn for the worse and she became confined to bed. One day in December 1951, on returning home from school, I was told by Mum that Grandma had been "waiting to see me" all day so I ran upstairs to her. We exchanged a few words, and I remember leaning across the bed to give her a kiss before going down again to have tea. A few hours later, Grandma was dead. Everyone said she had stayed alive by sheer willpower until I returned home from school so that she could say "goodbye" to me.

For the next four days, until the funeral was over, I found myself in a state of terror which I felt unable to share with anyone. The cause of my absolute dread was simply the fact that there was a dead body in the house. Grandma was "laid out" by Mrs Hodson, an old woman who lived near Dad's hen-pen and benefited from a supply of eggs. Her special gift and part-time job was making human corpses look presentable. Once she had called and used her skills, Grandma's body remained in the back bedroom (did someone mention "on planks on the bed"?) whilst friends and relatives came to pay their last respects.

As a fourteen-year-old I was not given the opportunity of taking part in this ritual, but had the offer been made I would have turned it down without a moment's hesitation. My fear became particularly acute at bedtime when, after saying goodnight to my parents, I had to go upstairs alone and pass the door of the room containing Dead Grandma before climbing the second flight of stairs to my attic bedroom. Once there, I was aware that midway between myself (in bed) and my parents (in the living room) lay a dead body — and upon this fact I seemed to focus all my fears.

Long after the funeral, the back bedroom remained for me a centre of unease and anxiety. I certainly could not have envisaged ever sleeping in it again as Maureen eventually had to do. I remember worrying about how I would cope when the time came for my own parents to die, and for many years I had a deep fear of death and dead bodies.

Perhaps the death of their mother drew Mum and Auntie Olive closer together for a while, for at about this time we had several invitations to visit Olive and Tom in their hotel in Scarborough. And so it was that during my early teenage years, when Maureen was about seven, our family made a number of journeys by train across the Pennines to stay at the Kingsway Hotel. It was like the coming together of chalk and cheese. Mum and Dad were essentially working class folk who were generally satisfied with their lot in life and whose main aim was to raise their family as well as possible on a very modest income. Olive and Tom were ambitious, wanted to become wealthy, and were easily dazzled by people whom they considered had status.

When we arrived, we were not treated as guests, but as "family". In effect this meant that Mum (in particular) gave considerable help with the day-to-day running of the hotel, and that our meals consisted largely of what was left over when the guests had finished theirs. Mum and Dad, always keen to contribute towards their keep, often bought bags of provisions from local stores which they handed in for general use, but Olive and Tom didn't seem to have the ability to make us feel at home or enable us to have an enjoyable holiday. On almost every occasion when we visited Scarborough, difficult situations arose or cross words were exchanged due to clashing values or incompatible personalities.

On a number of occasions, actors or singers who were appearing at one of the theatres on the promenade would stay at the Kingsway Hotel for the entire season. This not only gave Olive and Tom a great deal of kudos — "Oh yes, Jackie Allen and Barbara are staying with us, you know. Lovely people!" — but it was also a means of getting free tickets for the Summer Shows. On several occasions, we all went to the Futurist Theatre to see a "Showtime Spectacular", but the only person to pay out for tickets was Dad!

It was whilst I was at Scarborough that I became interested in fishing. I think it was seeing all the winkle and fresh crab stalls, and watching the experienced fishermen on the pier pulling in dabs one after the other that made me want to have a go. At first I had a rod, but soon realised it was not needed. Lots of shops were selling square wooden frames wrapped with a long brown line, so I bought one of those. At the end of the line was a metal weight and several inches above it were metal braces on to which were fixed nylon strands bearing hooks. All one had to do was to wait for an incoming tide and, after baiting each hook with a mussel or a lug worm, toss it into the sea and wait for a bite.

I must have spent dozens, if not hundreds of hours on Scarborough pier trying to catch my first fish. Whilst everyone around me seemed to be pulling in a flatfish every few minutes, all I caught was an occasional crab (much too small to eat) which had hung on to the bait whilst I lifted it out on to dry land. I only ever pulled in one dab — which had caught its gills on my hook as it was swimming past — and that was so small I felt duty bound to throw it back. Many years later, I learned why I had failed. The fishing frame I had bought was intended for taking out to sea on a boat to catch large fish such as cod, so the hooks fitted were much too big to go into the mouth of a small dab. However long I had sat on the pier I would never have been successful.

After a year or two, our family's trips to see Olive and Tom came to an end. On our final visit Dad returned home alone, and Maureen and I followed on with Mum a day or two later. On reflection now I think there had probably been a row and Dad had made the decision to leave early. I also seem to remember an argument between Mum and Dad on our return home, and Mum's words, "But she *is* my sister, Arnold," are still clear in my memory.

A few years later, Kingsway Private Hotel became Kingsway Holiday Flatlets. When flights abroad became cheap enough for the working classes to visit Spain, trade gradually fell away. Olive and Tom had to adapt to the situation and converted the premises. Several years later, they sold up. Although they eventually retired to a house in Torquay and were obviously not without money, the Doidges never became millionaires as they had hoped. And when Tom died unexpectedly, Olive was left a widow in unfamiliar surroundings and isolated from her family.

★   ★   ★

One aspect of life that caused me the greatest concern throughout my entire adolescence was my relationship with girls. During my earlier years I had had no trouble with them. Gwen Kershaw, who was one of our gang on Laneside, had been as tough and daring as the rest of us. But as I grew into my teens, girls took on a new dimension. They seemed to develop the power to simultaneously attract and terrify me. At grammar school, they gathered in small groups, whispered and giggled together secretly, pulled their navy blue cardigans across their rapidly developing chests, and in some strange way became mixed up with the taboo subject of sex.

Of course, the subject of sex — or anything remotely associated with it — could never be spoken of at home. Mum even found the word "love" difficult to say, and would bowdlerise it in conversations, frequently referring to young couples becoming engaged because they "liked" each other. In this climate it was impossible for me to have even the most basic discussion about sexual development. Whereas many parents of the day avoided the topic of human reproduction, they did at least speak to their offspring about boyfriends and girlfriends. In *my* case, Mum and Dad never mentioned the subject at all.

In the absence of all conversation on the matter, my knowledge of sex was gleaned (often inaccurately) from snippets of information picked up in the school playground, and a series of brief encounters with the opposite sex.

Although I no longer attended Sunday School on a regular basis, there were certain events held at Greenhill Chapel that provided opportunities for adolescent members to meet and mingle. One such event was the annual pantomime which was performed at Christmas time, and for which rehearsals began in September. Often, whilst older members of the cast were running through a scene on the stage, younger members of the cast would be running through the vestries, playing hide and seek and engaging in horseplay.

The games invariably involved a lot of chasing and catching and often when grabbing a girl around the waist, one might "accidentally" grab a little higher up. Whilst wrestling a ball off her during a game of pass-ball, one might "accidentally" fall and land on top of her, and spend a moment or two "wrestling" on the floor. These episodes were not seen as overtly sexual by the boys or girls taking part, but there was an element of excitement in the boisterous encounters and everyone engaged fully in the fun!

There are certain particular incidents that stand out clearly in my memory. On one occasion, after a pantomime practice, one of the girls was standing on a wall to look through a window. As I held her legs to support her, I suddenly became aware of their firmness and shape and recognised her "difference".

A year later, during a game of Postman's Knock at a friend's birthday party, I was gripped by a shapely young female and kissed on the lips, and I felt — for the first time — a ripple of excitement run through my body as she pressed herself close to me.

However, when it came to *sexual knowledge*, embarrassment and ignorance were the norm. At fifteen years old, I knew nothing about girls' periods or the menstrual cycle, I had no idea how babies "got out" at birth and had only the most rudimentary theoretical knowledge of how they got in there in the first place. Sex, instead of being a natural, wholesome thing, became for me, and many of my contemporaries, an exciting but unsavoury subject discussed by groups of misinformed boys behind the proverbial bike shed.

The consequence of learning about a fundamental aspect of life in such a furtive and haphazard way was most unhelpful. To begin with, it created an unhealthy fascination with all things sexual so that often I would thumb through books, magazines and encyclopaedias with the single aim of turning up words or pictures of a sexual nature. Teenage habits, through which I should have passed naturally, became obsessive and enveloped in guilt.

However, in spite of this preoccupation with the "*idea*" of sex, I did not have an easy relationship with girls of my own age. Whilst the subversive side of my personality spent a great deal of time in imagining ways of gaining carnal knowledge of certain attractive females, my conformist self was invariably tongue-tied in their presence and often had a faint suspicion that he was secretly being laughed at. Much of my time was spent oscillating between guilt and confusion.

★　★　★

perhaps I was so preoccupied with my own sexual development, and the uncomfortable feelings surrounding it, that I failed to notice a huge row blowing up in the family. For as long as I could remember, Grandma and Grandad Broome's house at Stubley had also been the home of my three maiden aunts, Annie, Florence, and Nellie. They all got on very well together and had their own individual friends, many of whom they had met at work. Nellie worked as a weaver and had a particular friend called Edith, who was her weft-carrier. Edith was often invited to the Broome household and became just like one of the family. Florence had a number of friends from Stubley Chapel where she worshipped every week. One of Annie's close friends was called Martha who was married to Maurice. She had known them both for many years, and often used to visit them at their house in neighbouring Wardle.

Sadly, Martha developed cancer in middle age and died after a long illness, but Annie went on seeing Maurice and eventually they formed an attachment to each other. By the time I became aware of the situation (as a fifteen-year-old boy) the two of them were going out together, and Maurice had asked Annie to be his wife.

Even though she was forty-seven at the time, when Annie announced her news to everyone, it had a similar effect to tossing a hand grenade into the family home. All sorts of objections were raised against the union. To begin with, Grandma and Grandad Broome had serious doubts about Maurice's suitability as a husband, because he was something of a "rough diamond". His language was rather coarse at times and, horror of horrors, he was thought to *"like a drink"* — which meant he made occasional visits to the pub. One could understand Grandma being somewhat anxious about this, but why Grandad (with *his* past) objected to the behaviour is something of a mystery. Then there was the fact that it was Maurice's second marriage, he had not been a widower for very long, and he was two years younger than Annie. In Grandma and Grandad's eyes, the whole relationship did not appear to be very seemly.

Nellie, on the other hand, was *absolutely furious* at the news. As their parents had got older, the running of the family home had tended to fall to the three sisters, but because Florence was a bit on the slow side, in actual fact it was Annie and Nellie who shared the housekeeping between them. Nellie saw Annie's decision to get married as abdicating her responsibilities and leaving her in the lurch, caring for two elderly parents and a retarded sister. She completely fell out with Annie and refused to speak to her for weeks. Tremendous rows followed, and on several evenings I remember Dad setting out to visit Grandma Broome's house with the intention of pouring oil on troubled waters. He had little success.

In spite of the opposition, Annie was determined to go ahead with the wedding and, encouraged by Mum and Dad and Ethel and Charlie, she and Maurice made an appointment at the Registry Office in Rochdale for 20th December 1952. Initially, Grandma and Grandad

Broome — spurred on by Nellie — said they would not attend the ceremony but they eventually relented and did so. Nellie stuck to her guns, however, and refused to play any part in the proceedings. On the big day, she stayed at home on the pretence of putting the finishing touches to the buffet which was set out on the dining table in the living room, but everyone knew that in reality she was registering her objections to the end.

After the ceremony, the wedding party returned to Stubley Brow and a quiet celebration was held to which family members and a few close friends were invited. Knowing of my interest in photography, Annie asked me to take some pictures, and using my system of photo-flash bulbs, wires and a battery I did so.

Eventually, things settled down again. Annie and Maurice moved into a small back-to-back cottage on Featherstall Road in Littleborough, about half a mile from the family home. Maurice turned out to be a very good husband, and within a year or so, all angry feelings had subsided and the rift had been healed.

There was one high spot at this time on which I look back with pleasure to this day. Since my earliest years, Grandad Broome and Dad had entered produce from their "hen-pen gardens" in the Littleborough Horticultural Show. As the annual event approached, they would select some of their best vegetables and flowers and prepare them for exhibition. Then, on the Saturday afternoon of the Show, the whole family would go to the Parish Church Hall to see how they'd done. The Show also contained a Children's Section, and local youngsters were invited to submit paintings of flowers or fruit that were judged and awarded certificates in a similar way to adult entries.

For many years whilst at junior school, I had won the first prize at this event, until Gerald Pickering, my friend from Calderbrook Road who gained a place at Grammar School a year ahead of me, managed to beat me into second place.

However, some years later, when I was fourteen, I came across an advertisement in the local newspaper inviting entries for the horticultural show which was held annually in the neighbouring town of Rochdale. This was a much grander affair. It was held in the magnificent ballroom of the stately Town Hall and a local celebrity or politician presented the prizes. The winner of the Children's Section in this Show received a silver cup to be held for a year by his or her school.

I determined to enter this competition and began work on my painting. What I did not realise was that entry forms had been sent out to all the Rochdale schools, and a large number of entries was expected, and eventually received.

When the day of the Show arrived, it turned out that mine was the only *independent* entry to have been received — and what is more, I had won first prize!

I walked on to the platform at the end of the crowded ballroom to receive the silver trophy from Mr Fred Loads, a well-known gardener and broadcaster, and took it home that evening with a sense of pride and satisfaction.

However, when I took the silver cup to Heywood Grammar School on the following Monday morning, there were few words of congratulation for me. As it happened, the school was outside the circulation area for the entry forms, so the head teacher and staff had no knowledge of the event. The head teacher accepted the cup from me when I took it to his study, but no mention was made of my success in assembly that morning, nor on any subsequent occasion.

Two days later, the trophy merely appeared on the high shelf alongside many others at the back of the school hall, where it stayed until the following autumn when the horticultural show came round again. There was no public recognition of my achievement and there were no words of praise to boost my self-esteem.

I made up my mind to leave school as soon as I was able, but as I was the oldest student in my school year, I was almost seventeen by the time I could do so. For five years I had ploughed through the grammar school syllabus, seemingly failing in most of the subjects, and had ended up with a grand total of four "O" levels. When it came to work, though, I had little idea of what I wanted to do. All I could think of was that I would like a job which was in some way connected with "Art" — probably because that was the only subject which I enjoyed and in which I excelled.

Of course, as far as my parents were concerned, I might as well have said that I wanted to fly to the moon. No one they knew, or had ever heard of, had made a living from being artistic, and they didn't know how to begin advising me on the matter.

And so it was that two weeks after I had made my final joyous exit from Heywood Grammar School, Dad and I kept an appointment to see the Employment Officer at the Youth Employment Bureau in the centre of Littleborough. I cannot be sure whether or not the man intended to be helpful, but his central message seemed to be that there were very few possibilities of employment in my chosen field.

The only firm he could think of which might possibly give me a job was The Calico Printing Association whose impressive premises stood in the centre of Manchester, and which had a textile-designing department. Should I have the good fortune to be accepted by them (which he hinted was unlikely) I would probably find myself making tea for several years before they let me anywhere near the designing studio. He made a future in "Art" sound very uncertain and precarious indeed!

However, after some consideration, he came up with another job that he thought I might find attractive. At that time there was a grave shortage of teachers. He wondered if I had considered returning to school to gain one more "O" level (making five) and then applying for a place at Teachers' Training College where I could train to be a schoolmaster?

Although I did not fancy the prospect in the least, Mum and Dad thought it was a wonderful idea. I would have the benefit of a higher education — and if there was one thing that could be said about teaching, they asserted, it was that it was a secure job with a regular monthly salary.

As I discussed the matter with my parents, I could feel my resolve to work in the art world gradually slipping away. I could find no arguments to prevail against the "common sense" view of having a "dressed up" job with a good salary. What other alternatives were there? I was too clever to end up "in the mill" (and in any case I did not want to do so), yet I had not shown enough academic ability to apply for university and get a degree. There *was* a possibility of taking an apprenticeship, but that was thought to be a waste of my grammar school education.

In the end, I gave in. On the first day of the new school year in September 1954, I made an appointment to see the head teacher of Heywood Grammar School and asked him if I might "sign on" for another year. By this time, I was seventeen years old, and even though I was re-joining the school as a member of the lower sixth form, I did not look forward to the daily journey on two school buses surrounded by hoards of noisy children.

For some time, I had been keen to purchase an autocycle, which was a cross between a cycle and a small motorbike. It looked like a heavy-duty bike with pedals, but also had a long, tubular petrol tank and small engine fitted below the crossbar. One great advantage of an autocycle was that the law at the time stated that a driving licence was not needed for vehicles with an engine capacity of under 100cc, and an autocycle's engine was rated at 98.

I suggested to my parents that the purchase of such a vehicle would be a good investment as I could travel to school on it every day, and it would also be useful for getting from place to place around Littleborough. After a little persuasion, they agreed to the purchase and, having seen one advertised in the local newspaper, I eventually bought one with their financial help.

It did not quite work out as planned. Although the journey of seven and a half miles seemed relatively short when travelling by bus, it felt an extremely long way when riding my autocycle. And even though traffic was much lighter in those days, I had little experience in negotiating roundabouts and crossroads, so my journeys were not exactly anxiety-free. In addition, not having appropriate clothing, when the weather was wet I got soaked to the skin!

However, by the following August, I had gained two more "O" levels, and had half-heartedly made the decision to become a teacher.

CHAPTER
SEVEN

23174839 Private Broome

The call-up papers came with my birthday cards, and although I'd been expecting them, their arrival still gave me a shock. Many of my contemporaries had sought deferment of National Service in order to complete courses of study, but it was the rule that those wishing to enter the teaching profession must first serve their two years in H. M. Forces. So as my birthday was in August, I had requested an "early call-up" in order to be released in time to start a teacher-training course (two years hence) in September.

It had never occurred to me that I would serve in anything other than the army. Never having had experience of military service, my parents and relatives had all made this assumption and I had never thought to question it. So when I attended the medical examination in Manchester and was asked which branch of the armed services I would prefer, requesting admission to the R.A.F. never entered my head. I discovered much later, when I arrived at college, that the overwhelming majority of my fellow students had spent *their* two years in the Air Force, and many had enjoyed the experience. For me, my time in the army was the most traumatic period of my life.

The day of my departure soon came. Eighteen years and three weeks old, a wide-eyed and still socially immature youth, I was driven to London Road Railway Station in Manchester by Uncle Charlie in his Austin Seven. Mum and Maureen waved me off from our front door in Calderbrook Road, and Dad accompanied me on the first leg of my journey.

The train left at midnight, and as it pulled away from the station my heart sank. I was going like a proverbial lamb to the slaughter. The only blessing was that I did not know the horror that was to come.

I was due at Portsmouth to begin my six-week basic training course at eight o'clock the following morning and I soon discovered that many of my travelling companions were making for the same destination. Conversations blossomed, anecdotes were told, and in one way or another we kept our spirits up as we journeyed along. Arriving at our final destination, we found a convoy of army trucks in the station yard waiting to take us to Hilsea Barracks. To the accompaniment of the yelling and bawling of the drill instructors, we scrambled into the backs of them — and the first day of my two-year sentence in the Royal Army Ordnance Corps had begun.

I was the youngest recruit in the intake, and without doubt one of the most green. Many of the others in my platoon were in their twenties; several were married; most had been in employment for a number of years. In short, none was quite so gauche and inexperienced as I

119

was. Six weeks earlier I had been a naive schoolboy —
now I had become a naive soldier.

It is not necessary here for me to go into detail about
the rigours of basic training, for this has been the
subject of many novels, films and television documentaries.
Suffice to say that I found the experience to be as bad
as the most condemnatory portrayal. We were sworn at,
harassed, humiliated, forced to change our clothes
many times a day, inspected, drilled and generally
demeaned in the name of military discipline. The single
objective seemed to be to break our spirits — and in my
case it was very nearly successful.

I remember the basic training course as a nightmare,
and my primary aim during those first six weeks was
personal survival. Although I had never been one to
write letters, I began to write home to Mum and Dad
on a regular basis — almost every day! In the desperate
situation in which I found myself, I wanted most of all
to keep in close touch with those who had reared me, in
much the same way as the chicks in Dad's hen-pen
scrambled under the mother hen when danger
threatened.

This pattern continued throughout the entire two
years. Several times a week I would put pen to paper to
let Mum and Dad know of my trials and tribulations,
and inform them when I was coming home for my next
36- or 48-hour leave.

My parents responded wonderfully. They wrote
letters giving me encouragement and support, telling
me of events that had happened within the family. They
sent me copies of "Radio Times" and the local

newspaper to keep me abreast of village news, and responded to my requests for food parcels with packs of goodies containing home-made cake, sweets, biscuits and fruit. At a time when I desperately needed their support, Mum and Dad went out of their way to show love and care.

During our basic training, we had a number of interviews in order that those in authority could decide on a suitable military career for each soldier, depending on his age, education and aptitude. As a result of this, after successfully "passing out", I was transferred to the School of Ammunition at Central Ammunition Depot, Bramley in Hampshire to train for nine months as an Ammunition Examiner. Although I did not appreciate it at the time this was, in fact, a good posting for me as it meant that I would be going to school again for the next nine months and on successfully completing the course would be awarded two stripes.

Although the camp at Bramley was set in beautiful countryside and the regime was less harsh than at Portsmouth, I still found it difficult to come to terms with the military lifestyle. We were billeted in "spiders" — long, low huts containing two rows of metal beds and green, steel lockers — clustered around a central ablution block. Here we spent the weekends and evenings whilst every weekday we were marched across the camp to the R.A.O.C. School of Ammunition. This rather grand title was given to the group of brick prefabs in which we learned to store, care for, and disarm various instruments of destruction.

On the day we arrived, we had just unpacked our kit and begun to place it in our lockers when the corporal in charge of our room shouted, "Stand by your beds!" at the top of his voice. Having just completed our basic training we were all well practised, and within ten seconds we were standing to attention in the approved position, eyes fixed on the opposite wall. In through the door, dressed in civilian clothes, strolled a young man, and as he entered the corporal marched towards him and saluted. The visitor then walked slowly up and down the room, glancing into the half-filled lockers.

"So you're the latest bunch of layabouts we've got to put up with," he sneered. "Well, I'm your Intake Officer, Lieutenant Pratt. You'd better watch out for me whilst you're here — I'll be checking up on the state of this spider when you least expect it. So if you don't want to end up on a charge — watch out!"

No sooner had our Intake Officer departed than another visitor arrived, this time wearing a dog-collar.

"I do hope you'll attend our services held each Sunday in the camp theatre," he said, smiling benignly and nodding to us all, "The Colonel in charge of our camp is a very devout man, and he will expect you all to be there every week."

When the minister of religion had left too, we all stared at each other in silence, convinced that C.A.D. Bramley was going to be even worse than our basic training. We had just sat down on our beds and begun to grumble about the situation when both our visitors burst in through the door again, doubled up in hysterical laughter. In reality, both were private soldiers and members of a previous intake who had only been at the camp for a matter of weeks themselves. With the collusion of our corporal, they had decided to play a practical joke on us all. I still find it amazing that they were not lynched on the spot!

However, in spite of lighter moments such as this, it eventually became obvious to me that the principles on which army life prospered were condoned bullying and sending the weakest to the wall. One example of this was the regular appearance of Sergeant Major Bell at the cookhouse door performing his infamous "mug inspection." If by chance he should find the smallest speck of brown tannin lurking in the corner of a soldier's mug as he entered the dining room, he would "accidentally" drop it on to the concrete floor where it smashed into a dozen pieces. After clearing up the mess, the luckless recruit would then have to buy a replacement from the Company Stores using his own money. The justification for this behaviour was that it saved us from being charged with the offence of having dirty equipment and so was "more compassionate". Personally, I think it illustrates clearly the sadistic nature of many in authority in the armed services.

The same Sergeant Major Bell also caused me to have one of my unhappiest weekends at Bramley, although I have to admit that in this case I was not entirely without fault. Soon after we arrived at the camp, we were issued with rifles (but no ammunition) which we had to keep in the green steel lockers next to our beds. As these were firearms, we were told that our lockers had to be kept locked at all times — and this was achieved in many cases by buying a simple padlock from the N.A.A.F.I.

Every day at 12.30p.m. we returned to our spider from our lessons at the school, and then made our way to the cookhouse for lunch. On one such occasion, I went into my locker for some item and then went for lunch, forgetting to re-lock it. By the time I returned half an hour later my rifle had disappeared and with fear and trepidation I asked our room corporal what I should do.

"If I were you, I'd go and report it to the Sergeant Major's office right away," he advised, "but I think it's likely they'll get you for insecurity of arms."

His prediction was correct. Although I reported the loss immediately, I was charged with insecurity of arms, and the following morning I had to parade before the Major. He handed down a punishment of "five days confined to barracks" (C.B.) which meant that I could not go home on the 48-hour leave which the whole camp would be enjoying during the coming weekend.

The punishment was annoying but not harsh. It involved parading in best battle dress at 6.00a.m. each morning with the retiring guard, and again at 6.00p.m. each evening with the guard coming on duty, and also at 10.30p.m. before "lights out". During the evening, duties (or "fatigues" as they were known) had to be carried out — often potato-peeling in the cookhouse kitchen. The real deprivation was not being allowed home for a leave that I had been looking forward to for several weeks. That weekend, in a camp usually occupied by several hundred soldiers, there were about thirty men maintaining its security of which I was one. I learned later that prior to each 48-hour leave, the Sergeant Major often "did his rounds", finding breaches of discipline in order to have enough men on C.B. to maintain the security of the camp.

It was whilst I was at Bramley that I experienced what in retrospect might be called a spiritual awakening. Before I was called up I had had little interest in spiritual matters, for although I had attended Sunday School regularly as a child, I had found the lessons boring and the Bible incomprehensible.

The only interesting period was soon after the war when a fighter pilot returned from the Air Force and was persuaded to take one of the Sunday School classes. We managed to get him to spend the lessons in describing his own exploits in the air, rather than God's interventions in the world. But when he left and the Superintendent replaced him, the boredom quickly returned.

By the time I was drafted into the army, the Almighty had become an irrelevance. I rarely gave him a thought. Nevertheless, when I first got to Portsmouth, one of the many things that shocked me was the low moral climate in the barrack room. The bad language positively lit up the air, with strings of profanities and blasphemies illuminating the most mundane remarks. And the other men's descriptions of sexual encounters with women who apparently "couldn't get enough of it" had my eyes popping out of my head.

At first, my own language remained moderate — as it always had been at home — but eventually, influenced by the degenerate atmosphere, I slipped into swearing and was soon as bad as all the others.

When I arrived at the Bramley spiders, I was allocated a bed next to a chap called Ted Mellor. Ted was a most unlikely soldier. Whereas most of us had spent time in shrinking our berets by dipping them in hot, then cold water so that they hugged our heads, Ted was content to let his hang down one side of his face to well below his ear. And whilst many of us had had our battle-dress blouses tailored to make them a better fit, Ted's uniform remained as issued, and looked about two sizes too big for him. In consequence, he had the general appearance of a khaki-coloured sack of potatoes.

Because he was my "neighbour" in the barrack room, I had many conversations with Ted. He was in his mid-twenties, lived in Uttoxeter, and was engaged to be married. But two things stood out which distinguished him from the rest of us. The first was that he never swore, and the second was that every night he knelt down beside his bed to pray. The reaction of the other squaddies in the hut to this behaviour was predictable — the sight of a pyjama-clad figure kneeling at his bedside was too good an opportunity to miss and gave rise to many a ribald comment. At times, he was teased unmercifully.

Although initially I thought Ted's behaviour was rather odd, his integrity and sincerity gradually got through to me. He said little about his faith — other than that he was a Christian — but I found myself admiring his determination to follow his conscience in such a hostile environment. Within a week or so, I was swearing less often myself, and before a month had passed I had given it up altogether.

Later, I began to attend "Padre's Hour" which was held in a small room set aside for the purpose in the camp and, accompanied by a couple of friends, made occasional visits to a chapel in Bramley village. Sometimes we were invited out to tea by members of the congregation and spent evenings in their homes. For the first time in my life, the work of the church seemed to have some relevance, and attending services seemed worthwhile.

The nine months at the School of Ammunition passed quickly, and were prompted by monthly tests that we had to pass to remain on the course. Those who failed were entered on a parallel but easier course and ended up as Ammunition Storemen.

Our tutors on the course were sergeants and the occasional officer — regular soldiers who spent their days teaching successive intakes of National Servicemen. Unfortunately for me the methods they used were similar to those of my grammar school teachers, placing emphasis on rote learning and memorisation. So once again my level of attainment left something to be desired. When the course ended and the final test had been administered, I found myself in my usual position — categorised as one of the poorer students in the group.

At the end of the Ammunition Examiner's Course, all successful participants were promoted to the rank of corporal and allocated to camps in various parts of the country which held stocks of ammunition. With a surprising regard for democracy, the colonel in charge of the School decided that each recruit should be allowed to select his own posting from the available vacancies depending on his success in the final exams.

The camps nearest to my home were at Nesscliffe, close to Shrewsbury, and Longtown, not far from Carlisle — and at first it appeared that I might be successful in gaining a place at one of these. However, at the last minute, a couple of soldiers above me in the list decided to change their minds which meant my only choice became Central Ammunition Depot, Corsham near Bath, the camp which on the grapevine had the worst reputation of all.

Although deeply disappointed not to be moving nearer to home, there was nothing I could do but make the best of it. So I focused on the fact that almost a year of my National Service had already passed, and things surely couldn't get worse than they had been.

On arrival at Corsham, I was surprised to discover that the ammunition was stored underground in the old Bath stone mines — and that this would be my place of work. During the winter months I would be below ground during all daylight hours, descending before dawn and returning to the surface only after darkness had fallen.

Whilst at first this seemed rather daunting, in truth I soon found that life underground was not half as bad as it sounded. There were subterranean canteens and toilets which catered for our physical needs, and we worked alongside local "civvies", many of whom had growing families of their own and were only too pleased to "show us the ropes" and help us in any way they could.

Even so, I have always blamed the working conditions at Corsham for the fact that I took up smoking. Before going underground, all soldiers and civilians had to pass through a guardroom in order to deposit packets of cigarettes, lighters or boxes of matches in personal lockers. Regular random searches were made by the guards to ensure that this iron rule was observed and anyone found beyond the gate in possession of smoking materials was subject to severe punishment.

On returning to the surface however, the first act of most soldiers was to light up and enjoy their first cigarette for hours, and many non-smokers, unable to experience such joy, felt they were missing out. I was amongst them, and soon succumbed to the habit, little realising that it would take me many months of effort ten years later to break the addiction.

It was whilst I was at Corsham that I became addicted to my special "Corsham Diet" on which I survived for close on thirteen months. As soldiers working underground, at lunchtime we had the choice of either returning to the surface for a meal prepared by army cooks and sent in containers to a prefab close to the entrance, or we could pay for our meal and eat in the underground civilian canteen. Having tried the former for a while and been very unimpressed, I decided to settle for the latter.

Although it served only a limited menu, the civilian canteen was much better in every way. To begin with, it was not subject to military discipline so had a more relaxed atmosphere, and as it was located just a few hundred yards away underground, the long trek to the surface was not necessary. The choice of food was very restricted, consisting of a number of pies and a selection of crisps and chocolate biscuits, but was served by motherly women who gave everyone a friendly smile and an encouraging word. After a few days of experimentation, I decided on my favourite combination — a steak and kidney pie and a "Wagon Wheel" (which was a very large chocolate biscuit with a butterscotch filling). So every workday for the next year or so, my mid-day meal consisted of these two items. And I can honestly say that never once did I become tired of the choice!

As Ammunition Examiners, we spent our days in blast-proof "work areas" built from sand-filled ammunition boxes, and set at intervals in the miles of underground passages. Our work was of three types:

- testing small random samples from stacks of shells or mortars to ensure that stock was not deteriorating;
- doing a full stack inspection where there was doubt about its condition, and
- carrying out various "special jobs" which arose from time to time.

One such "special job" that occupied me for several months was the testing of fuses fitted to the noses of

25-pounder shells. Several of these had been found to have corroded internally, causing them to explode in the barrel of the gun when it was fired, so our task was to "drop-test" the entire stock. The procedure was not difficult and its name was most appropriate. It involved dropping each fuse in turn down a metre-high drainpipe on to a concrete block. If it did not explode, it was in good condition!

Periodically, there was a little more excitement in our lives. Now and then an item of ammunition would be discovered in a very dangerous condition. It could be anything from a box of rusty hand-grenades to a single shell with a badly corroded fuse. When this happened, dealing with it was designated as a "one-man risk" job and the item was sent above ground.

Once on the surface, it was taken to a small hut in the middle of a field where a single Ammunition Examiner was detailed to make it safe. These "one-man risk" jobs always seemed to come up on Saturday mornings, and in retrospect I am not sure whether the risk was quite as grave as it was made out to be — but at the time it added a little spice to our lives. Although I was only called upon once to take the lonely walk out to the little hut, I found it to be quite a daunting and knee-knocking experience.

The Suez Crisis happened whilst I was at Corsham. We all awoke one morning to find the barrack square filled with sand-coloured lorries, each containing a sleeping driver. Initially, we could not understand what they were doing there, but we soon found out! At our Morning Work Parade, we were informed that a

24-hour shift rota would be operating from the following day and all leave would be suspended. It was of paramount importance that ammunition was shipped to our troops who were waiting to go into action.

For the next week or two, everyone at the camp — Ammunition Examiners, Ammunition Storemen and members of the Royal Pioneer Corps — spent day after day underground loading boxes of ammunition on to the conveyor belts which took them to the surface and the waiting lorries. In the event none of it was used, and several months later it all came back again to be taken underground and re-stacked. But by that time I was within days of my release.

After what seemed like an eternity, the day I'd been waiting for eventually arrived. Early in September 1957, I walked out of the camp at C.A.D. Corsham a free man. The feeling of relief, excitement and exhilaration which I experienced is difficult to describe. I almost *skipped* along the road to the station — it was as though a great burden had been lifted from my shoulders. After two years in purgatory, I was sure that anything that followed was bound to seem like heaven.

My future was already planned. During my time at Bramley I had gained a place at Didsbury Teachers' Training College in Manchester, and was due to start on a two-year course in three week's time. After a few days of joyful celebration, I settled down to some serious shopping and bought myself a briefcase, ring files and pens.

But I never returned to Laneside. Whilst I had been in the army, my parents had managed to save enough money for a deposit on a new home. They had moved out of the rented, end-terraced house in Calderbrook Road where I had grown up, with its communal backyard and shared toilet, and had taken out a mortgage on a property in Newall Street, nearer to the centre of Littleborough. Here they had superior accommodation — downstairs a sitting room, a dining room, a kitchen and a pantry under the stairs. Upstairs there was the luxury of a bathroom with toilet, and three bedrooms, including one in the attic. They also had a private backyard containing their own dustbin and coal shed.

I began my course at Didsbury Training College at the end of September, and was resident in college for the whole of my two-year course. After my service in the army, college life was indeed a pleasant and relaxing experience — and it was there that I met my wife-to-be Anita Stanley. Eventually, I passed out as a fully qualified primary teacher in 1959, and was married in 1961 at twenty-three years of age.

Since that time, over forty years have passed and much has happened. I completed a career in primary education, working in four schools in the North of England and eventually becoming the head of a small Church of England Primary School in Middleton, Manchester. Anita and I had two children, David and Lisa, and we now have two grandchildren, Jack and Molly.

★ ★ ★

In retrospect, I realize that my parents were honest, well-meaning people who were loving and supportive and full of integrity. In spite of their idiosyncrasies they provided a stable home environment for my sister and me, demonstrating care in practical ways when we were ill, and supporting me with letters, gifts and regular food-parcels when I was feeling miserable and isolated in the army. I am very grateful to them for the care they gave and feel fortunate to have been their child.

I remember with affection, too, all my relatives and friends who provided the wider environment and encouraging framework in which I was able to develop and exercise my independence.

I can honestly say that I have never regretted my Northern roots.

Also available in ISIS Large Print:

A Pennine Childhood

Ernest Dewhurst

Dad farmed on a slope. If I'd lived at Tum Hill for a lifetime I might have developed a slant.

Ernest Dewhurst was brought up on a small Pennine farm between the Pendle Witch Country and the more distant Brontë moors. This is an affectionate and self-deprecating look at his life at home on the farm, of family and friends, school and chapel, and the excitement of travelling fairs and Christmas "do"s.

On leaving school, Ernest became a local newspaper reporter, against the backdrop of war. His wartime stories include the Home Guard "invading" Burnley and he and his father being mistaken for spies. The book ends as he is called up "to hinder the Royal Navy".

ISBN 978-0-7531-9396-9 (hb)
ISBN 978-0-7531-9397-6 (pb)

Before the Last All Clear

Ray Evans

*Except for Mam and Dad, none of us had ever been
out of Liverpool before, never mind on a train.*

This is the story of one young boy from Liverpool,
whose family was sent to the Welsh town of Llanelli for
the duration of the war. Separated from his mother,
and brothers and sisters, six-year-old Raymond Evans
was shunted form pillar to post. At first he had a
miserable time, unwanted and largely unloved, and it
appeared that his war would be spent without any
family — real or surrogate.

Ray's world is one of ration books, black-out curtains,
air-raid sirens and sudden death; a world in which
humanity triumphs despite its own shortcomings.

ISBN 978-0-7531-9380-8 (hb)
ISBN 978-0-7531-9381-5 (pb)